BLACK-BELT
JUDO

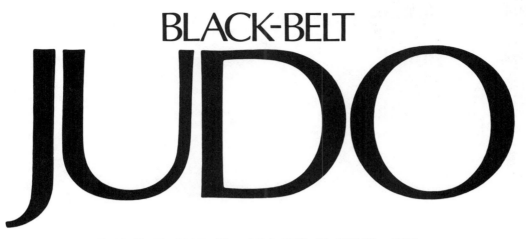

BLACK-BELT
JUDO

GEORGE R. PARULSKI, JR.
5th DEGREE BLACK BELT (godan)
TECHNICAL ADVISER: ISAO OBATO
7th DEGREE BLACK BELT (shichidan)

ENDORSED BY:
**THE AMERICAN
SOCIETY OF
CLASSICAL JUDOKA**

**THE ALL-JAPAN
SEIBUKAN MARTIAL
ARTS AND WAYS
ASSOCIATION**

CONTEMPORARY
BOOKS, INC.
CHICAGO

Library of Congress Cataloging in Publication Data

Parulski, George R.
  Black-belt judo.

  Includes index.
  1. Judo.   I. Title.
GV1114.p36   1985   796.8'152   84-23286
ISBN 0-8092-5326-7

Original *sumi-e* illustrations by Carolyn Parulski.

Interior photography by Carolyn Parulski.

Cover photography by Rich Russell (RR Photographic Services)

Published by Contemporary Books, Inc.
180 North Michigan Avenue, Chicago, Illinois 60601
Manufactured in the United States of America
Library of Congress Catalog Card Number: 84-23286
International Standard Book Number: 0-8092-5326-7

Published simultaneously in Canada by Beaverbooks, Ltd.
195 Allstate Parkway, Valleywood Business Park
Markham, Ontario L3R 4T8 Canada

Dedicated to the loving memory of
Leonard Iachetta—
friend and father—

   Who left us too soon,
   Too abrupt,
   Too heartbroken

Through your loving example
   we have lived on.
Although I did not know you long enough,
   I am content to have called you Dad.
May you find peace in the universal *tao*.

and

To
Louise Iachetta,
Who lives in his memory and
Love.

CONTENTS

ACKNOWLEDGMENTS

The author expresses his sincere thanks to the following people and organizations: to the Manfredi School of Karate, run by Peter Manfredi, for use of its facilities during the photo session; to Phil DiCasolo, executive director of the Bayview YMCA, for allowing us to use their Nissen mats for the photo session; to Carolyn, a better wife a man will never know, who took all the photos that appeared in this text; to Rob Horowitz and Bill Rourke, for posing with the author for the many photos that appear in this book; to Isao Obato, for consenting to be the technical advisor of this text and for his sincere help and dedication to this project; to Instant Photo for their fine job in processing the black and white photos; to Akira Tazawa and his father, Shizuo Tazawa, for assisting with the cover illustration on this book; and to Jody Rein, my editor at Contemporary Books, Inc., for having the keen insight to seek the publication of a technical book of this nature. Through her insight, *The Complete Book of Judo* and *Black-Belt Judo* stand as the finest books available in print on the "Gentle Way."

FOREWORD

As a mirror is necessary for us to maintain our physical appearance, such as shaving, combing our hair, applying make-up, etc., so advanced techniques, especially the formal exercises (*kata*), are indispensable for our judo practice.

A mirror is necessary not only for careful appearance but also for maintaining our health. *Kata,* which is the systematic formulation of the most fundamental principles of throwing, grappling, and body attack, can prevent us from prostituting the purity of true judo.

It may be said that all other throwing techniques and grappling methods are only modifications of those fundamental techniques of kata. Kata, then, is not practiced necessarily for direct sport or self-defense application, but rather is used to instill in its practitioner the fundamental *spirit* or *essence* behind a particular concept.

Without a doubt, the kata is the most fundamentally important practice in judo and is also the most neglected. Because kata are difficult to learn and execute and are not always immediately applicable to contest situations, they sometimes are neglected or, worse, never studied at all. Methods of advanced throwing which are not applicable in a contest are left behind. Similarly *Atemi-waza,* the methods of hitting, are almost forgotten. I can remember when the karate chop was called a "judo chop." But all too often, the sport of judo prostitutes the purity of genuine classical judo. Not too long ago, judo was respected as an effective means of self-defense as well as a sport. Too often today the sporting egos have left judo an empty shell, devoid of its martial heritage.

This is partly the reason for the formation of the American Society of Classical Judoka. Through this organization, the true art of judo can be promoted and preserved.

There has long been a cry in judo circles for a manual that would deal with the more complex elements of judo; however, up to now, those cries have gone unanswered. *Black-Belt Judo* gives the *judoka* a complete guide to the advanced levels of true judo.

The author, George R. Parulski, Jr., is one

of the most gifted judoka I have ever met. With his vast knowledge and abilities in Japanese *Budo* (martial ways) and his flawless judo techniques, he has once again created a masterpiece in martial arts literature.

With his first volume, *The Complete Book of Judo*, which covers the entire area of basic judo techniques for competition, and his *Black-Belt Judo*, which covers advanced judo methods in great detail, George Parulski has in fact created a two-volume encyclopedia the likes of which the world of judo has never seen and will probably never see duplicated so professionally.

Both his volumes are fully endorsed by the American Society of Classical Judoka as being the finest judo books available today.

Isao Obato
7th Degree Black Belt (*Shichidan*)
Technical Advisor for *Black-Belt Judo*
President/founder
American Society of Classical Judoka

Summer 1984
Arizona

INTRODUCTION

The completion of *Black-Belt Judo* is the culmination of a dream: to produce in two volumes the most complete material available on the true art of judo—not just the sport, but the entire field.

This dream began in 1984 with the publication of *The Complete Book of Judo* (Contemporary Books, Inc.), the most complete book of judo basics available in print. With *Black-Belt Judo* it is my hope that the judo world will discover once again the true values of judo when it is practiced as a martial art rather than as a game. This author has no complaint with judo being practiced as a sport, nor with the AAU. My point is that true judo—as it is practiced by the silent majority—is a complete martial art, involving but not limited to sport judo.

Perhaps of greatest interest in this text are the judo kata. Handed down for centuries from the great Japanese masters and considered to be the crucial link with the past, the judo kata—or "formal exercises," as they are translated—are the customary and classic fundamental movements involved in attack and defense. They are rooted in the ancient art of *jujutsu* and have been refined and improved to reach their present high state. Katas reveal underlying principles and, on a higher level, spiritual knowledge of ourselves and our environment.

Black-Belt Judo addresses the advanced concepts of judo in four major sections: Background, Theory, and Conditioning (Part I); Throwing and Locking (PartII); Kata of Judo (Part III); and Self-Defense Techniques (Part IV).

In Part I we examine the history of judo in the light of jujutsu. Unlike my first book *The Complete Book of Judo*, which relates the history of judo through the eyes of the *Kodokan* (main judo headquarters), this book gives new insight into the meaning and purpose of judo by looking at it through jujutsu, judo's predecessor.

The theory covered in Part I also represents a different approach from that of my first book. This time we look at judo as an expression of Zen and how to make the concept of *mushin* (no-mind) work for you.

While Dr. Kano, judo's founder, exemplified the concept of *mushin*, he never specifically addressed it as it is addressed in this book.

In Part II, we take judo a step further by looking at some of the less popular throwing methods. They are less popular not because they are ineffective, but because they are seldom used in competition. In examining the locking/holding techniques, we discover that judo is indeed a formidable method of self-defense. These techniques, prohibited in competition, represent the more lethal aspects of judo. Also in this section is a look at *ne-waza* strategy. This is aimed at the competitive judoka (judo player). All too often I am asked, "How do I get into a hold-down?" Well this section should answer questions like that one. In order to prevent turning the section into a chapter on wrestling, I have presented only those techniques found in judo but not in wrestling.

Part III examines the *Nage-no-kata* (forms of throwing), *Gonosen-no-kata* (countering methods), *Kime-no-kata* (forms of self-defense), *Itsutsu-no-kata* (forms of five), *Koshiki-no-kata* (forms of antiquity). I have selected these five kata (out of 13) as being representative of advanced judo theory.

Finally, Part IV is intended to give the reader a complete look at judo as a true method of self-defense. These methods are the *Atemi-waza* (striking/kicking techniques). At first look they appear to be a form of karate, but in reality they existed long before karate became an organized martial art.

This author acknowledges the help of Master Obato for his technical assistance with this book. Through his careful study of the manuscript, corrections were made to make this the finest book on advanced judo technique in print.

George R. Parulski, Jr.
5th Degree Black Belt (*Godan*)
USA President
Dai-Nippon Seibukan Budo/Bugei-Kai
(All-Japan Seibukan Martial Arts and Ways Association)

Summer 1984
Webster, New York

ON USING THIS BOOK

Although this book on the advanced techniques of judo is intended to be a companion to *The Complete Book of Judo* (Contemporary Books, Inc., 1984), picking up where the first book left off, I have taken great care to make *Black-Belt Judo* stand on its own feet, independent of other volumes. Nonetheless, to get the most out of this book, you should have a working knowledge of basic judo theory and philosophy, know the *gokyo-waza* (techniques of 50) throwing system, and have a working ability in general *ne-waza* (ground work) methods. The techniques in this book will take you through brown belt and into the black belt ranks.

If you do not possess the prerequisite knowledge, I suggest you do read through my first book, *The Complete Book of Judo*.

Throughout this book, references are made to terms and techniques for which more information is given in *The Complete Book of Judo*. Such information is flagged by footnote numbers. The footnotes appear at the back of the book and indicate which pages in *The Complete Book of Judo* contain further information on each subject footnoted.

PART I:
BACKGROUND, THEORY, AND CONDITIONING

Softness will overcome hardness,
Weakness will overcome strength.
All things that yield
Will control those that do not
Give in.

Lao-tzu
Tao-te Ching

1
FROM JUJUTSU TO JUDO:
AN HISTORICAL OVERVIEW

Modern judo is commonly called a sport, a martial art, a way of spiritual harmony, a system of physical education, and a recreational activity. To some extent, all these definitions are accurate. Judoka completely dedicated to the art consider it a way of life but a full appreciation of the true nature of judo is yet to be attained by many of its nine million or so exponents. This is because the scope of judo has frequently been viewed too narrowly; many of its important cultural aspects have been played down in favor of a few specialized ones.

In order to see judo in its fullest light, it is necessary to look at the origin of Kodokan judo, its rise from the art of jujutsu, and the personal motivations of its founder Dr. Jigoro Kano.

HISTORICAL BEGINNING OF JUJUTSU

It is safe to assume that self-defense is a natural instinct that exists in everyone. This being the case, there is probably no country in which the art (whatever its form or name) of fighting another unarmed is unknown. However, in no country has the art of unarmed fighting made such great strides and progress as it has in Japan.

Feudal Japan saw many methods of combat wax and wane. *Jujutsu, tai-jutsu, yawara, wajutsu, toride, kogushoki, kempo, kumiuchi* were just a few. Of greatest concern to us are the methods of unarmed combat called jujutsu (also called *jiu jitsu, jiu jutsu, jujitsu*).

Opinions differ widely as to the origin of this martial art. One theory traces jujutsu to Chin Gempin, a naturalized Chinese; another theory champions Shirobei Akiyama, a physician at Nagasaki who, it is stated, learned three tricks of jujutsu-type combat in China; still another theory claims jujutsu is a product of Japanese ingenuity.

Concerning the first theory, Chin Gempin became a naturalized Japanese subject in 1659 (d. 1671). Studying at the Kokusho-ji monastery in Azabu, Tokyo (then Edo), Chin Gempin is said to have taught three *ronin* (masterless samurai or "wave men") three "tricks" (techniques) of jujutsu. These ronin were Shichioyenmon Fukuno, Yoiyemon Miura, and Jirozayemon Isogai. After much analysis of the methods taught them, each of them founded his own *ryu* (school or system). Most scholars of Japanese martial arts history agree that the "tricks" taught to these ronin were methods of *ate-waza*—striking and kicking the vulnerable areas of the body. Since jujutsu is not an art based entirely on *ate-waza* (although it does play a major role), it would be wiser to assume that Chin made a significant contribution to an art already in existence.

Now to the second theory, which states that Shirobei Akiyama is the father of Japanese jujutsu. Akiyama is belived to have learned jujutsu-type methods in China and taken them back to his country. Upon examination of this theory, we find that Akiyama did indeed learn a martial art in China, but it was in the forms of *hakuda* and *kempo*. Both of these arts stress kicking and striking and contain few throwing or grappling techniques. It is therefore highly doubtful that jujutsu originated with Shirobei Akiyama. It should be noted that Akiyama's role in founding jujutsu is acknowledged by the *Shinyo-ryu* jujutsu schools and not the entire jujutsu community.

The third theory, that jujutsu is a product of Japan, is perhaps the soundest of the three. It is important to understand, however, that the role of Chinese influence in jujutsu is an important one, for without this influence, jujutsu never would have matured. Still, it is important to establish the fact that jujutsu-type combat existed in Japan long before the Chinese influence was felt, for it thereby proves that *jujutsu* originated in Japan. Proof of this can be found in the book *Kuyamigusa* (*My Confessions*), which was published in 1647, 12 years *prior* to the immigration of Chin Gempin. In this text, references are made to *yawara* and *kumiuchi*, two terms that are synonymous with *jujutsu*. The term *kumiuchi* is also found in many books predating the *Kuyamigusa*. Further, the oldest established jujutsu system in recorded history, the *Takenouchi-ryu*, existed well over a hundred

years before the arrival of Chin Gempin in Japan.

In fact, if we look more closely at the history of Japan, we find much evidence of the existence of unarmed fighting arts. The earliest verifiable culture of Japan flourished circa 5000 B.C. (*Jomon* era). *Haniwa* (clay figurines) of warriors from this period that illustrate jujutsu-type fighting stances and grappling techniques have been found in neolithic tombs.

The first written documentation we can draw on for reference is the *Kojiki*, written by Opo-no-Yasumaro and commissioned by Empress Gemmei on 18 September, A.D. 711. In the *Kojiki*, it is reported that "Opokuninushi (Great Land Ruling God), the champion of Amaterasu (Sun Goddess/Grandmother of the First Japanese Emperor), combated the rebellious warrior Takeminakata-no-Kami and defeated him by catching his arm, locking it, and immobilizing him as he was tossed to the ground" (Book One, Chapter 36).

Further evidence of the early existence of jujutsu-like systems is found in the *Takanogawi*, a Shinto book. It tells how two gods, Kashima and Kodori, grappled with one another and later used jujutsu-type techniques to stop rebellious tribes that lived in Japan's eastern provinces.

Of less mythological content is the *Nihon Shoki*, a chronicle that appeared in A.D. 720. The *Nihon Shoki* is a written account of the events that took place in 23 B.C. The work records how Emperor Suinin ordered two strong men, Nomi-no-Sukume and Taimano-Kuehaya, to wrestle in his presence. After fighting, which consisted mainly of kicking, the former gained the advantage and finally broke the ribs of his opponent. Elated by his success, Nomi went to the great length of trampling—and breaking—the loins of his vanquished competitor, which ended fatally for the latter. The *Nihon Shoki* is generally accepted as demonstrating the origin of Japanese wrestling (*sumo*). However, considering the fact that Kuehaya was kicked to death with the aid of grappling techniques, it seems that the contest consisted more of jujutsu techniques than of sumo.

Later, Emperor Syomu, A. D. 742–749, instituted the official rules of combat for future martial arts contests. His successor, Emperor Kammu, A. D. 781–806, built the *Dai-Nippon Butokukan* ("Great Japan Training Hall for Martial Arts") in Kyoto in A.D. 782. With the year A.D. 792 came the formation of the *kondei*, or "stalwart youths"—the forerunners of the samurai. These youths trained themselves exclusively in *bugei* (martial arts), and by the reign of Emperor Minmyo, A. D. 833–856, annual *bugei* contests were being held in the land.

With this rich heritage of combat came specialization. It is recorded that a method of grappling was devised by Teijun Fujiwara, the sixth son of Emperor Seiwa Fujiwara, A.D. 850–880. It was passed down in the family until it was revised and improved on by General Shinra Saburo Yoshimitsu Minamoto. Under him, this family system was called *Daito-ryu* after the noble gentlemen's seat of residence.

THE GOLDEN AGE OF JUJUTSU

Although the history of jujutsu can be considered to have begun somewhere in the second century B.C., the "Golden Age" of jujutsu occurred during the Tokugawa era, A.D. 1603–1867. During this period, Japan attained peace following a century and a half of war. Tokugawa performed the sensitive task of maintaining a unified country by keeping the *daimyo*, the feudal barons who controlled large portions of land, weak. He did this by requiring each daimyo to spend alternate years residing in Edo (Tokyo), the new capital. To give them the proper incentive, he kept their families as permanent "guests."

With this unification came peace. And during this time of peace, the number of fighting arts flourished. There were some 725 recorded systems of jujutsu alone, the most popular being the Takenouchi-ryu, Jikishin-ryu, Yoshin-ryu, Sekiguchi-ryu, Kito-ryu, and Tenshin-shin'yo-ryu. The last two jujutsu ryu were instrumental in judo's subsequent development.

Let us take a closer look at the major jujutsu schools of the era that have survived to this day.

TAKENOUCHI-RYU

The founder of this school was Hisamori Takenouchi, a native of Haga village in the province of Mimasaka. Takenouchi was a religious man who kept a vigil at the Sannomiya Shrine. While in religious observation, he practiced with a *bokken* (wooden sword) with a length of three feet six inches, slamming it against a large tree. He did this night after night until he was exhausted. One day before falling asleep, a *yamabushi* (warrior priest) appeared in front of him and taught him five arresting techniques, as well as the advantage of small weapons over large. The art of arresting later came to be called *kogu-shoku*, and to this day it has a rather large following.

YOSHIN-RYU

This school was founded by Shirobei Akiyama, a physician in Nagasaki. It is said that Akiyama learned three modes of *hakuda* (striking) and 28 types of *kappo* (jujutsu art of resuscitating) in China and that on his return from China he taught them to his students. He was not impressed, however, by his own efforts and by the shortcomings he found in his progressing art. He went into meditation for 100 days, hoping to come up with a solution to his dilemma. On the last day of his prayer, a heavy snowfall occurred, and many trees had either their trunks or limbs broken under the weight of the snow. In the midst of this scene stood a single willow tree, which was so pliant that the snow was unable to accumulate on it. With this lesson, Akiyama invented 300 jujutsu "tricks" and called his school, *yoshin* ("heart of the willow").

SEKIGUCHI-RYU

This school was founded by Jushin Sekiguchi, whose ancestors were related to the powerful Imagawa family of Suruga province. In his younger days, Imagawa was very devoted to the arts of swordsmanship and jujutsu. It wasn't long before he had become a master of both and earned fame throughout Japan. Based on his own interpretation of the art as his ancestors knew it, Jushin founded Sekiguchi-ryu.

It is through jujutsu's involvement that judo reached its high standards of technical proficiency. Through use of proper methods of control, the jujutsu locks and control holds can render an armed opponent harmless.

KUSHIN-RYU

This school was founded by Nagakatsu Inoye. Inoye first studied the jujutsu of the Kito-ryu school under Takino in 1717. Having earned a good reputation in Edo (Tokyo), Inoye added his own personal interpretations to Kito-ryu and devised a system he later called Kushin-ryu.

KITO-RYU

The Kito-ryu is a system that traces its roots to the famed Chin Gempin, who taught three ronin three methods of Chinese grappling and striking. The system was founded by Kanyemon Terada, a retainer of Tango-no-Kami Kyogoku. Terada studied the art under Fukuno, one of Gempin's three ronin, and later perfected the art to its highest standards.

Kito-ryu concentrates on what many call a hard, yet yielding, approach to combat with extra emphasis placed on throwing techniques and kata (prearranged exercises). Kito-ryu exists to this day in a slightly updated form. However, the original concepts of Kito-ryu are forever preserved in the judo kata *Koshiki-no-kata* (see Chapter 11).

TENSHIN-SHIN'YO-RYU

Based very much on the concepts of yielding and of circular energy, this art is described both as an *aiki*-jutsu system and as a system of jujutsu. (Aiki-jujutsu, or aiki-jutsu, is the art of "inner harmony.") The art manipulates an opponent's oncoming force, turning it against him either to project him (throw) or to immobilize him (pin). The art is based on the circular dissipation of an enemy's force, or *aiki*. It is believed that the concept of aiki was derived from *ken-jutsu*, or swordsmanship. The most famous aiki-ju-jutsu schools are the Daito-ryu and the Ten-shin-shin'yo-ryu. The art was founded by Matayemon Iso, a retainer of the Kii clan. A native of Matsuzaka in Ise province, Iso, as a boy, studied Yoshin-ryu jujutsu under Oribe Hitotsuyanagi. At the death of Oribe, Iso studied *Shin-no-shinto-ryu* jujutsu under Joye-mon Homma. Becoming a master in the latter style, Iso set out to search Japan for more systems to study and match his considerable skills against all other jujutsu and aiki-jujutsu systems. It is said he never lost a match. During a visit in Kusatsu (Omi province), Iso with the help of his student, Nishimura, encountered 100 criminals who were bent on destroying a local village. With his use of aiki and atemi (striking), Iso defeated the entire crowd. This taught him the importance of aiki methods as well as the necessity of strik-ing and kicking (something that was being ne-glected in jujutsu circles). He founded the Tenshin-shin'yo-ryu based on these prin-ciples.

THE MEIJI RESTORATION AND THE RISE OF JUDO

The *bakumatsu*, or end of the *bakufu* (Sho-gun's tent or military government), was a period of final decay for the Japanese feudal military regime established by Ieyasu Toku-gawa in 1603. The bakumatsu was caused by the changing domestic and international con-ditions under which the shogun (military dictator) could no longer keep the nation effectively segregated from the outside world.

The growing unrest caused many daimyo to coerce the shogun to return the power of the country's government to the emperor. This brought about the Meiji Restoration, when the hollow structure of the shogun's bakufu crumbled and the Meiji emperor as-sumed control of Japan in 1868.

The so-called architects of the restoration proposed a little national cleanup. Their in-tention was to sweep away more than 700 years of imperial impotence, during which Japan had been ruled by a succession of pow-erful families, including the Tokugawa.

The Meiji government began to take dras-tic measures to reconstruct Japan. The pro-gressives saw the need to do away with many feudal institutions, especially those that fa-vored returning the government to pre-To-kugawa ethics. The clash of the progressives and the conservatives resulted in a convulsive course of politics that was punctuated by actual combat.

The Charter Oath, a declaration made in the name of the emperor in 1868, became the platform for the Meiji government. The last of the five articles is significant: "Knowledge shall be sought throughout the world so as to strengthen the foundations of the imperial rule." This article was interpreted broadly to mean *fukoku-kyohei*—"a prosperous nation with strong dedication to government and all parts (people) working for the whole."

Along with this idea came an almost na-tional revulsion for the budo (martial ways) of the Tokugawa era. Tokugawa budo were personal and spiritual; they were for the good of the self, not the good of all (government). They lacked *fukoku-kyohei*. Therefore many budo were unofficially banned. The govern-ment did not in essence ban the practice, but in order to adapt to *fukoku-kyohei*, the Japanese ceased their practice of budo/bugei. Jujutsu fell into disuse. The top jujutsu men of the era were giving strongman demonstrations in the street in order to survive financially.

In order for feudal budo and bugei to sur-vive the Meiji Restoration, they had to be-come a tool to make their practitioners into better people *for the good of all*. In many cases, budo reverted to bu-jutsu (warlike tech-niques rather than arts for spiritual cultiva-tion) or else entered the realm of physical education and sport. Sport was for the good of all as well as the good of the one. It therefore was a means of achieving *fukoku-kyohei* without losing personal identity.

Thus, the term *sport* meant more than it does today in America. Sport was complete physical education; it was not just a game. Techniques for killing and defending were still included in the training, but now the emphasis was on using them in a holistic manner, by training mentally, physically, and spiritually.

It is to the credit of Dr. Jigoro Kano that jujutsu survived the Meiji Restoration. He took his beloved jujutsu and altered it to adapt it to the times. He called his new methodology *judo*.

JIGORO KANO

Jigoro Kano was born in 1860 in the seaside town of Mikage. His family moved to Tokyo in 1871 to advance their economic standing. Kano's first taste of martial arts came through a family acquaintance, Ryuji Katagiri, who later convinced the teenager to join the Tenshin-shin'yo-ryu under master Fukado in 1877.

Under the guidance of his *sensei* (teacher), Fukuda (who was a student of Iso Mateyemon, the founder of the system), Kano began his long journey to physical well-being. The Tenshin-shin'yo-ryu was a hard/soft style of both aiki and jujutsu that, during the Meiji period, did not stress combat but instead stressed harmony. However, the ryu still had an excellent reputation for producing fine fighters.

The specialty of the ryu lay in its use of *ate-waza* (striking), *katame-waza* (holding), and *aiki* (circular dissipation of force) methods. Kano's injuries were numerous during the course of his training—but still he continued.

When his teacher died, Kano joined the Kito-ryu jujutsu under the direct supervision of Iikudo Tsunetoshi. Tsunetoshi's brand of Kito-ryu was much softer than Kano's previous experience with jujutsu (however, Kito-ryu in *general* is noted for its hard defensive tactics and throwing methods). Tsunetoshi stressed *ran*—"freedom of action"— and only moderately strenuous workouts. Attention was instead paid to abstract symbolism connected with physical technique. Kito-ryu stressed nage-waza (throwing) and effective self-defense "tricks."

After many years with the Kito-ryu, Kano began a comprehensive study of other jujutsu, including *Seigo-ryu* and *Sekiguchi-ryu* (among others). Kano then began the self-appointed task of making jujutsu a part of the national culture.

He started this task by involving himself in the educational system and in politics. Eventually, Kano found himself with a seat on the newly founded Japanese *Diet* (parliament). By 1879, Kano decided it was time to update jujutsu and make it a part of the Meiji philosophy. He initially felt that it was important to create the strongest syllabus from among the various jujutsu schools. In doing so, he named his art *judo*, a term he took from the *Juikkishin-ryu*. To distinguish the two, he used the adjective *Kodokan*.

The term *Kodokan* breaks down into *ko* (lecture/study/method), *do* (way/path), and *kan* (hall/place/school). Thus *Kodokan* means "a place to study the way."

Up until this point, Kano was teaching his art of Tenshin-shin'yo-ryu for master Fukuda, and in 1879 (just prior to Fukuda's death) Kano and Fukuda gave a demonstration of Tenshin-shin'yo-ryu to former U.S. president General Ulysses S. Grant, who was then visiting Japan as a guest of the Meiji government.

Following Fukuda's death and Kano's study of Kito-ryu after his teacher's passing, Kano started the first Kodokan school in 1892 at the Eisho-ji Monastery.

By 1885, Kano began to work toward a philosophy of a martial art form (judo) that, as far as was possible, eliminated the risk of injury for the practitioner. Kano was accepted by the jujutsu community not because he was establishing his own methods, but because he was teaching a blend of Kito-ryu throwing techniques (nage-waza) and Tenshin-shin'yo-ryu striking and circular locking techniques. To these were added the techniques of many other systems. This was accomplished by many jujutsu masters of the era, who taught their methods through the Kodokan.

Historically, it is important to keep in mind that Kano did not want to dismember jujutsu and replace it with a sport form of benefit only to the nation. Instead he wanted his Kodokan to be a hall in which all jujutsu masters could preserve the techniques of their ryu, for the good of the people (Meiji aim). His judo was an educational tool for the good of the spirit, intellect and body. Because it was a tool for education, sport play did figure largely in its usage, but this was only a small part of judo's aim.

Dr. Kano established a three-fold path: body, character, and intellect.

Body: Kano observed that the body is the instrument of life. Therefore, the body is the temple of existence. The necessity for physical fitness, then, is self-evident. The physical aspects of judo train the body to its fullest capacity, and the sporting (*shiai*) aspects of judo—*when correctly applied*—give the body character.

Character: Kano said, "We live in a world of humans; we must therefore follow the rules of humans. If we lose our desire to live as humans, we lose our worth." Judo is a method of developing sound character. Proper training teaches us the principles of life.

Intellect: "Intelligence builds character," Kano preached. Thus, it is all-important to develop the intellect as well as the body and character in order to be a complete human being. Judo is also a means of building the intellect; it offers determination and self-discipline to learn all that one can in *all* aspects of existence.

The philosophy of body, character, and intellect brought about harmony with oneself and one's surroundings. Harmony was further explained in a concept Kano called *kyushin-do*. Kyushin-do (or *kyoshin-do*) is a precept of judo with three maxims: *banbutsu ruten*—all things in the universe undergo a succession of changes; *ritsu-do*—rhythmic and flowing movement (how judo techniques should be done); and *cho-wa*—all things work and flow in perfect harmony; therefore in practice one should have harmonious mental and physical reactions in a given situation.

For some reason that seems to escape historians, the Kodokan began propaganda campaigns to support the fact that the new Kodokan judo was superior to all existing jujutsu systems.

Some point to an incident in 1886 between the Yoshin-ryu jujutsu school of Dr. Baelz and the Kodokan, which were great rivals. Finally, a contest between the two schools was arranged. It was held at the Central Police *dojo*, with 15 men representing each side. Kano made up his team from his top students as well as the jujutsu masters who taught their arts through the Kodokan. One such master was Shiro Saigo, a master of Daito-ryu jujutsu (an aiki system). The result was 13 to 2 in favor of the Kodokan. Over the years, the people of the Kodokan pointed to this contest as a means of showing judo's superiority over jujutsu.

Because of such propaganda, Master Saigo left the Kodokan in 1891 and went to Nagasaki, completely forgetting both jujutsu and the Kodokan.

In 1900, however, judo suffered a sound defeat by the *Fusen-ryu* jujutsu. Up to this point, the Kodokan had concentrated only on standing techniques (*tachi-waza*), and when judoka were taken to the *tatami* (mat) they lacked *ne-waza* (ground work) skills. Thus, in 1906, Kano instituted *katame-waza* (grappling) methods in his syllabus. Also, in 1906 the Dai-Nippon Butokukan (All-Japan Martial Arts Hall) announced the formulation of the formal exercises (*kata*) of judo.

Although it is true that Kano had won the hearts of some jujutsu masters and the contempt of others, his judo played a great role in jujutsu's survival. Because of the Kodokan's earlier propaganda campaigns against jujutsu, which, one should note, were later abandoned (some believe they started to help judo gain a firm support in the Meiji government, which in turn was for the good of all), many masters of jujutsu who were not affiliated with the Kodokan felt that Kano had abandoned many of the basic teachings and precepts of jujutsu.

Others, specifically those who supported and helped Kano (and knew what he was doing firsthand), felt that judo was a necessary evolution for the good of all *budo*. It is not surprising that the same basic views are still argued today.

The Kodokan became an official Japanese foundation in 1909, and two years later, in 1911, the Kodokan Black Belt Association was formed. In 1921, the Judo Medical Society was born.

Dr. Kano's efforts were not limited to judo but extended over many horizons. Dr. Kano helped many other sports enter the country, and he has often been referred to as the "father of Japanese sports."

In 1935, he was awarded the Asahi prize for "Outstanding Contributions in the Fields of Art, Science, and Sport." Three years later, he went to the International Olympic Council meeting in Cairo, where he succeeded in getting Tokyo nominated as a site for the 1940 Olympics.

On his way home from the momentous conference, aboard the S.S. *Hikawa Maru*, Jigoro Kano died from pneumonia at the age of 78. The date was May 4, 1938.

His treasure and his contribution to the world were his high ideals and his high values for judo.

TODAY'S KODOKAN

Today, any person, regardless of age, sex, or nationality, may be enrolled as a member of the Kodokan Institute. The main practice area has 500 mats, 100 feet by 100 feet, with several smaller areas including offices and dormitory facilities. It is located at #20 2-chome, Kasuga-cho, Bunkyo-ku, Tokyo City. The All-Japan Judo Federation and the International Judo Federation have offices in the same building.

2
ADVANCED THEORY:
THE ART OF ZEN IN JUDO

The Zen student Tokusan used to go to master Ryutan in the evenings to learn the secrets of Zen and the concepts of no-mind (mushin). One night it was very late before Tokusan had finished asking his questions.

"Why don't you go to bed?" asked Ryutan.

Tokusan bowed and lifted the screen to go out. "The hall is very dark," he said.

"Here, take this candle," replied Ryutan, lighting one for the student.

Tokusan reached out his hand and took the candle.

Ryutan leaned over and blew it out.

The student never returned to the master, for in that simple act he comprehended the concept of no-mind.

The philosophy of Zen has slowly found its way into the hearts of many Americans. Today it is not unusual to see judoka of all ages meditating in the dojo (gym) or "gazing at a wall" to wake up their true nature. The judoka looks to Zen to gain inner strength (ki) and understand the inner working of his art; the meditator looks to understand himself; and the everyday American looks to Zen to understand and handle the stress of modern-day society.

In short, many are seeking but few are finding. Some say that few Westerners understand Zen because of the culture in which they are reared. But eminent Zen scholars, like D. T. Suzuki, disagree with that. The reason few are enlightened by Zen is not cultural; rather, they lack fundamental understanding and proper instruction.

The importance of Zen study to the judoka only becomes clear at the point where the particulars of physical technique are left behind and it becomes obvious that there is something besides simple muscle memory that makes judo a martial *art*. Zen training has always been of interest to martial artists because it offers a way of disciplining the mind that eventually allows the practitioner to deal freely and appropriately with the demands of his art. The judoka who wishes to progress beyond physical technique should familiarize himself with several key concepts of Zen training.

One of the most important aspects of Zen for the judoka is *mushin-no-shin*, or mind-of-no-mind. Unless no-mind is truly comprehended, the judoka will never benefit from Zen and will miss an important heritage of his art.

The concept of no-mind is not simple to understand, yet ultimately, it is simple. To grasp no-mind is to grasp reality and the secrets of true budo. When no-mind is attained, all is possible: the meditator finds his true nature, the judoka gains nearly superhuman insight and a sixth sense, and the everyday American finds peace, even amidst society's tension.

It is extremely difficult to find an English term that adequately translates mushin. It is perhaps easier to describe the experience.

Any judoka who has practiced for a while can remember at least one special time when a technique worked incredibly well. It seemed to take no effort to perform it and when asked how it was done the judoka honestly has no recollection of the details. It just seemed to happen. The judoka's state of mind during that technique was the no-mind.

No-mind is not a concept, but an experience. The theories that have built up around it are only an aid to further practice. Zen training itself is not an intellectual exercise but an attempt to point the student directly at the experience itself. Because it speaks so directly it became a useful tool for all walks of life: the samurai warrior applied the principles of Zen to make him invulnerable on the battlefield, and the Zen monk used the principles to bring him the secrets of the universe.

The most important concept of Zen is the idea of self-nature and how to bring about enlightenment (*satori*/the final goal). But self-nature is not to be perceived as something of substance. It is not the last something left behind after all things relative and conditional have been removed from the mind. It is not self, soul, or spirit as they are ordinarily regarded. It is not something belonging to the category of understanding. It simply cannot be described in any way, but without it our everyday world collapses.

In the traditional terminology of Zen, self-nature is emptiness (*sunyata*) or the Unconscious with a capital U.

When Zen speaks of the Unconscious, it steps beyond psychology. The unconscious of psychology is a sort of storehouse where products of the mind have gone, and may come up again, sometimes with impelling or persistent force. It has been called "lapsed intelligence" or "sub-conscious." The Unconscious of Zen, though, is not some limited part of our self. It is the totality of our being. It is our self-nature. It is called the Unconscious because most of us have a very limited egocentric view of what we are. We are "unconscious" of our self-nature.

When a state of true no-mind is attained, our Unconscious is revealed to us. In a sense we become "conscious of the unconscious," and we realize that our everyday habits of thought are only a small part of ourselves. This awakening has to be taken for fact that goes beyond argument. The bell rings; its vibrations are transmitted through the air. This is a plain fact of perception. In the same way, the realization of the Unconscious is a matter of direct experience, as in the achievement of the black belt as a result of physical practice. No mystery is connected with it.

Philosophically, the concept of no-mind is deep, but without truly understanding it, the judoka will never completely master judo (in the traditional sense of judo as a Way). It is the concept of no-mind, one should note, that has attracted most of the interest in Zen. The samurai, or feudal warrior of Japan, looked to Zen as a way to still his fear of death and to help him, through direct application of no-mind, gain a sixth sense that helped him predict an opponent's move before it was actually executed.

The sword then was not a weapon but an instrument to help unite the mind and body. The mind and body could be united only by applying the concepts of no-mind.

Kyudo, or Japanese archery, is not a sport in which one is concerned with hitting the target. Instead kyudo is concerned solely with drawing the bow and releasing the arrow in a state of no-mind. The bow and arrow are only catalysts in helping to achieve a state of no-mind. In this respect, so is the sword.

Mushin literally translates as "without

heart" or "without mind." This leads to two definitions: (1) complete cutting off of the thought streams, and (2) freedom from unnecessary thoughts while engaged in some activity.

The first definition can be misleading. One tends to interpret the idea of "cutting off" as the absence of thought—like deep sleep or total annihilation. However no-mind is not a brainless stupor. Zen attempts in its practice to wrap discursive thought and feelings into one bundle and then remove it from the mind. After this has occurred, the mind is left with itself, or its self-nature. When the judoka can see from this source, his movements become those of a master.

Mushin, in the second definition, does not mean no thoughts; it means no inner reverberations of thought. It is the condition of being free from unnecessary thoughts when engaged in things of this world so that there are actions but no inner reactions. Some masters refer to this form of mushin as a sneeze. You do not make up your mind to sneeze; you simply sneeze. Although you can check the sneeze, one usually doesn't; you simply go ahead and sneeze. People who hear this are often quick to ask: "Do you build a house without thinking? Don't you plan where to put it, what materials to use, etc.?"

Mushin, in regard to this, does not mean no thinking. The location of the house, its plans, and its materials are considered, but there is no anxiety, no ambition, and once the due consideration is over, they are forgotten. To compare this directly to judo, one cannot enter a combat situation thinking, "I will do this or that to my opponent." What if the opponent does not move in such a way as to allow you to apply your preconceived fight plans? No! It is best to enter a combat situation in no-mind, being reflective enough to respond instantaneously to whatever the opponent throws at you.

For the judoka to aim at achieving no-mind is useless, however. As the old Zen saying goes, "You cannot wash off blood with blood." Likewise, you cannot remove thought with more thought (i.e. conscious effort). Mushin is not annihilation of awareness, though it cuts off thought; it is compared to a vast clear sky with no clouds in it.

At the beginning of monastic Zen training, the master often instructs the student to lie still for long periods of time. For a good time the beginning student is full of internal impulses to keep shifting. Eventually, however, these give way to calmness.

This exercise is intended to show the student how much effort is expended to continue even the smallest of body movements. Once the student has a sense of that effort, he can eliminate unnecessary movement in favor of stillness.

In the same way, thinking of meaningless thoughts at first appears natural and inevitable, and to drop such thoughts takes effort. After much training, such thoughts are regarded as mere mental twitches, and the Zen student begins to feel the benefits of mushin.

Mushin means doing things without casual thoughts about profit or loss or what you must do to obtain what belt rank. Mushin also signifies, and more correctly is described as, a state of mind alert and aware of itself but without a thought. In this state, the judoka becomes the art—his actions are in harmony with it.

For a student of judo, mushin makes up the greater framework of mental and spiritual understanding, with several other principles coming out of it, or benefiting from mushin. Today's judoka, being caught up in achieving belts and trophies, lack fundamental understanding of these basic judo principles. For this reason I present them as follows.

RI AND JI

Although common terms in Buddhism, these words are used in judo to mean an entirely different concept. *Ri* refers to inspired movement; it signifies an insightful feeling into the true nature of judo, the space-time relationship, and the moral situation. The true inner ri is most clearly manifested in feelings of beauty and power. To do something *muri* is to be without ri. Muri can be seen, therefore, as forced results, using unnatural and wasteful, tiring means. To throw an opponent with leg power alone, instead of with the whole body with coordi-

The concepts of Zen in judo create what is termed a *Calm Mind* that can remain reflective and open, able to, at an instant, respond to an armed attacker and put him completely under one's control.

nated movement, or to pull someone to the ground, rather than using off-balancing (*kuzushi*) methods, would be examples of muri. To do things in ri is to be at harmony with them.

Ji refers to technique created by the masters. Ji and ri are inspirations of the past. If they are mere imitations, they lose touch with ri; situations change constantly and so should technique.

Mushin allows ji to exist with ri. Ultimately, the master judoka will allow the technique (ji) to be standard, yet through mushin it maintains a part of the master's personality. When a technique (ji) is executed, it is done with inner feeling (ri) and is totally adaptable to the situation (ji/ri) and wastes no movement, being of no-mind.

SHIN AND KI

Shin is the Japanese term for heart, including all we attribute to the mind. *Ki* is vital energy. When executing a throw, shin is the notion of doing it, including the emotional coloring behind it; ki is the feeling of initiating movement and making sure that the movement conforms to proper distance and timing.

When shin is pure (from no-mind), thoughts do not arise from selfishness or passion, and inspiration passes through it. Without the condition of no-mind, shin becomes distorted and dark. Such questions arise: "Will this technique work for me?" "What shall I do if it doesn't work?" Without no-mind in shin, the shin is unsure and cannot adapt to the situation at hand.

When ki is pure (with no-mind) it adapts. At times of stillness ki fills the body and is at peace. Prompted by shin at the time of action, ki is in touch with cosmic energy. When ki is without no-mind (impure) it is slow and useless. When you should be still, you will instead be nervous; when you should be ready to defend yourself, you will be confused and thus defeated.

No-mind, because it is a state of no preconceived thoughts in a situation of life and death, will allow the judoka to adapt instantly to the situation at hand and achieve his ultimate victory. It is like the budo concept of *mizu-no-kokoro* (mind like water). The mind should be empty, like the still (empty) surface of the water. This way it reflects all around it as it really is. However, when a pebble strikes its surface (thought entering the mind as to what to do in a given situation), the surface is distorted and the images reflected by the surface are distorted. True reflections (assessment of a situation) are impossible. Only by keeping the mind reflective (no-mind), like the still surface of the water, can you be guaranteed of victory.

ISSHIN AND ZANSHIN

Isshin (one heart) means to throw oneself totally into the situation at hand without any thought at all. *Zanshin* (remaining heart) means that there is still some awareness remaining.

In judo, isshin is to commit one's body completely to a technique. If the technique is defective, or the opponent more skillful, it will miss. However to remain in zanshin is to keep awareness, which is wide and unmoving and contains the isshin. The immediate awareness is thrown into action, yet something remains (zanshin) that can handle failure as well as success. Zanshin, however, will not work if it is conscious thought. It must arise from no-mind.

Do not set the mind. Simply put, the judoka cannot set his mind on one technique; doing so would mean defeat. The mind must be allowed to flow freely from one technique to another, flowing like the waters of a stream.

If the flowing is stopped (the mind tries to think of a particular technique), the result will be a general stiffness and confusion. The wheel will revolve only when the shaft is not too tightly attached to the axle. If the mind is not in a state of mushin, the judoka will not be able to hear, nor will he be able to truly see, even when light flashes before the eyes or when sound enters the ears. Keeping a technique in the mind will force the mind to stop functioning. However, by remaining in a state of reflectiveness (no-mind), the judoka will be aware of what technique to use at the instant it is required.

UKEMI (FALLING)

Ukemi, in this context, does not refer to ukemi-waza methods to prevent the body from being injured when hitting the mat. Falling has both a mental and a physical meaning. Physically, when a drunk falls, he is not hurt because his body is relaxed and his mind is calm. By remaining in no-mind, the body and the spirit are less likely to be hurt when sustaining an attack. Should your defenses fail, no-mind can still keep you out of trouble.

Mentally, falling refers to falls in life. Judo, like life in general, is a road upward, always feeling and seeking a goal. To be able to take failure with the whole personality and then leave it behind is the mark of a master. The Zen adage says, "Fall seven times and get up eight."

The road to understanding and mastering judo takes many paths. For the traditionalist, the principles of Zen and no-mind are essential to mastery of his brand of martial arts.

THE CALM MIND: MEDITATION AND JUDO

Those nearing the level of black belt, as well as beginners interested in philosophy, have probably heard the expression "Empty your mind so it will reflect." Yet few understand the meaning of the words, and still fewer know how to make the words a reality. The "calm mind," an expression for a collection of philosophical ideas, is an attempt at explaining relaxation, harmony, reflection, and unity of the human mind, body, and spirit.

The idea of the calm mind began way back in India under the guidance of Hindu and Yoga masters. However, the concept was perfected through Zen Buddhism and later found perfect application in the hands of the great *budo* (martial ways) masters.

Success in acquiring a calm mind is based on (1) an understanding of the philosophy of Zen and mushin, (2) the techniques of meditation, and (3) a complete understanding of the physical technique.

You also must be able to:

Look in a detached manner, using the senses to their greatest sensitivity;

See without intellectual analysis of what is going on but with intuition and feeling; and

Feel an opponent's move without actually seeing it coming.

To be able to look, see, and feel, a judoka must be in tune with his inner self. You cannot achieve this by practicing the physical (for indeed Dr. Kano stressed meditation as a tool for better physical techniques), nor does it require you to live at a Zen monastery. Basically, a handful of knowledge and the idea of the meditative aspects of training, mixed with devotion, are all that is needed to attain a calm mind.

You cannot achieve it by saying "Yes, I have it." It is not something tangible, nor can it be achieved overnight. Like the physical perfection, the mental aspects of judo take as much, if not more, time to master.

The first step in the realization of the calm mind comes with an understanding of Zen. Zen itself is unique. It therefore defies classification and makes description all but impossible.

The word *Zen* is a corruption of the Chinese *Ch'an*, which comes from the Hindu word *dhyana*. It is said that Zen is a method that is a "vigorous advance up the mountainside without recourse to the well-worn but far longer paths which ultimately reach the same enlightenment."

Zen was founded by Bodhidharma, an Indian monk, during the Liang Dynasty. But the concept of the calm mind came to perfection under the guidance of Hui-neng, A. D. 638–713, Zen's 6th patriarch. Born in the Hsiu-cho province of Southern China, Hui-neng was required to start work at an early age and was unable to complete his education. One day, when passing a temple, he heard someone reciting a Buddhist scripture. The words deeply touched him and, after earning enough money (to support his mother), Hui-neng went to the temple to apply for admittance.

At the monastery Hui-neng studied under the fifth patriarch, Hung-jen, and soon became his favorite student. When Hung-jen announced that he would be looking for a successor, everyone assumed that his oldest pupil, Shen-hsiu, would become the next patriarch. When asked by his master to compose a poem to show his insight, Shen-hsiu wrote:

> The body is the Bodhi-tree [wisdom tree],
> The soul a mirror bright;
> Take heed to keep it clean,
> and let no dust collect upon it.

All who read these lines were sure that Shen-hsiu was to be the next master. However, the next day in the meditation hall, this poem appeared:

> There is no Bodhi-tree,
> Nor a mirror bright;
> Since all is calm [void],
> Where can the dust alight?

When Hung-jen read these words he knew the author matched his insight into the concept of Zen. He passed the partriarchy to the author, Hui-neng.

In those few short lines, Hui-neng perfectly outlined the basic concept of the calm mind. However, the greatest obstacle in discussing the meaning of Zen and its relationship to the calm mind is the difficulty in explaining exactly what Zen is and how it works.

To know and understand Zen—even to develop a basic understanding of it—requires practice and meditation. To reach a state of illumination (the goal of Zen), it is necessary to follow certain definite techniques. One is a form of question and answer that is shared between a master and a pupil, with the ordinary thought process speeded up to the point of abrupt breaking into awareness. This is called *mondo*, and since it is totally dependent on a teacher, we will not concern ourselves with it here.

The second technique is called *koan*, a formulation in words that often seem senseless to the rational mind, a veritable riddle. Thirdly, there is *zazen*, or seated meditation, often practiced in the judo dojo. Here one's thoughts are quieted so that one's original "essence" will break through, plunging the student into awakening or the state of the calm mind.

To work on the Zen riddle, koan, one must have a sense of sincerity and enduring eagerness to solve the riddle, but also (and here comes the twist) one must face it without thinking about it. The koan will contain key words, or "seeds," that are intended to break open the sealed door of our ordinary consciousness.

To relate this to judo, you must understand that the technique itself is the koan, and its application is likened to the riddle. If you use it (a technique) as a means to unite yourself with yourself, you will go beyond the physical and into the realm of harmony. This is what Dr. Kano meant when he referred to judo as *kufu*, or naturalness in physical movement.

Again and again, the koan shows us that we cannot take hold of reality by abandoning the false; nor can we reach peace of mind or any final answer to the koan through mere logic—just as we cannot hope to win in battle by *thinking* of what to do next.

Once you have taken up this ancient question of meaning, you are on your way to an impasse, which your so-called rational mind cannot solve for you. It is at this point that the Zen koan acts as a sort of explosive to break the blockage. But one cannot explain a koan; koans are meant to be directly experienced.

Examples of koans you can ponder follow.

"Zen is nothing but he who asks what Zen is."

OR

"The cherry tree blooms each year in the Yoshino Mountains. But split the tree and tell me where the flowers are."

OR

"If my own true being has nothing to do with birth and death, what am I?"

OR

"What is judo?"

By throwing your mind at these riddles, you can break through the logical barrier of thought, helping the mind act from intuition or, in short, achieving a calm mind. Once the mind can be intuitive with a koan, it can do so in other situations, namely combat.

Those who feel uncomfortable with a written koan can replace it with a physical koan such as a judo kata. By physically and mentally throwing yourself into the kata/koan, you force the body to act without reason and to defend without thought.

Far less obscure than the koan aspect of Zen, zazen, or seated meditation, requires less philosophical endurance and can be practiced in the dojo along with the physical aspects of judo. Meditation (zazen) is a way of getting in touch with the inner self. It forces you to transcend your everyday way of perceiving, thinking about, and relating to the world around you. Psychologically, meditation allows us to comprehend a new image of ourselves: our inner selves. This realization will bring a strong sense of serenity and inner peace, causing us to remain stable, even in the face of much adversity.

Meditation then, is not a regression, but rather an undoing of our *old* self to get in touch with the new spirit. The crayfish sheds its rigid shell when more space is needed for growth. The judoka, through meditation, may also temporarily cast off the shell of automated perception and get in touch with his inner power. Meditation was the secret of the samurai's power and *is* the secret of the great judo masters.

The experience of meditation and the Zen path is the attainment of a new reality and the accomplishment of a calm mind. But don't take this writer's word for it, nor that of the hundreds of judoka who have tried to convey this experience. Go out and search and practice for yourself.

The best way to get started is to select a place of meditation. This can be any room or the dojo. Seat yourself in a meditative posture,[2] always with back, neck, and head straight. *Listen!* Simply close your eyes and listen to the world around you. Take in all its hum and chatter. Don't identify any one sound with its origin; simply listen to the sounds the ears want to hear. Do the same with thoughts entering the mind. *Do not resist them or force them out.* Treat them as you treated general noise.

After a while (and with much sitting and practicing) you will discover a silence even amid the loudest noise. The next step is to control your breathing.[3] Try to breathe in six times a minute, counting to five on inhaling and to five on exhaling. (Breathe from the pit of your stomach and not your chest.)

Sitting in this tranquil state year after year, the student will rise above the world of the senses and experience a bliss and tranquility that cannot be explained in words. It is through this bliss that we discover the calm mind, the state the great judoka taught but few have attained today. The key to all meditation, however, is not in philosophizing but in *experiencing*.

MEDITATION TECHNIQUES

There are several other techniques that the student might try while seated in meditation (for a complete look at these techniques see my *A Path to Oriental Wisdom*, published by Ohara Publications, Inc., 1976). The following are the most advantageous to judo training.

THE ONE-POINTED METHOD

The essential point of this meditation is to look at something actively, alert, and without the aid of words. Pick an object to work with and look at it intensely, trying to feel it (as if you were using your sense of touch to feel a soft material). The object, at first, should be an item from nature: a pebble, twig, or even an autumn leaf.

Let me give you an example. Take a pussy willow and stroke it, feel it, smell it. Do this for about 30 seconds. Now look at the object. Really penetrate the object with your eyes, feeling it in the same way you did with your hands. For most people, there are two distinct feelings: that of touch and that of sight. When we use touch, our senses bring the stimulus directly to the mind, where there is no confusion or doubt. When we use sight, the stimulus is translated into words, not tangible feelings. By practicing this concentration of staring at an object, we learn to *feel* with our eyes. Thus, when we look at our opponent, we don't just see him; we penetrate him.

Once you have mastered this part of the exercise, the next step is to draw the object into yourself. In Zen this is called fixed meditation.

When you learn to draw the object into your mind, you will feel yourself grow lighter and more aware as the object's energy passes through you. This one-pointed method was conceived by Zen master Takuin and taught to the 17th-century master swordsman Yagyu-no-Kami Munenori, who referred to the technique as the secret of his success. Yagyu credited the one-pointed technique with his ability to see through the opponent and *feel* with his eyes the actions his opponent was going to take (even before the opponent himself knew).

BUBBLE MEDITATION

In this meditation, picture yourself sitting quietly on the bottom of a clear lake. Picture each bubble that rises to the surface of the water as being representative of each thought, feeling, and perception. When you have a thought or feeling, observe it in this manner until the bubble is out of your range. (Remember, a bubble is clear, and you can see from one end to the other. In this way, you not only see your thoughts but also see through them.)

This is a very structured meditation that teaches the judoka to rid himself of thought. Once the mind is rid of thought, consciousness is reflective, like the twilight moon that shines over all. In this state, as in the One-Pointed Meditation, the student is trained to remain calm in the face of attack and to anticipate assault.

For the true judoka, the road to and through black belt is a quest for truth. The calm mind lies at the center of the mental experience and should be sought by all. Until the judoka learns to unite his mind, body, and spirit, he will never move like a finely tuned machine, nor will he be at peace with himself. The drama of the martial spirit is enacted within the rhythm and the cadence of a song. Some sing it well. Others will never learn its meaning and therefore never find its melody.

3
STRENGTH CONDITIONING

The greatest asset a judoka has in addition to his mental development is his level of physical conditioning. Judo ranks number two in overall physical development (cardiovascular fitness, musculoskeletal fitness, and flexibility) according to a recent study of physical activities conducted by the Hopkins Institute. (Running is number one.)

A number of specialized judo flexibility exercises[4] and yoga exercises[5] are taught to the beginning judoka. However, as you progress up the ladder of rank, you soon realize the need to increase your muscular strength, not necessarily your muscular mass (the latter is a personal preference, not a necessity).

There are a number of specialized exercises that judo incorporates to promote greater strength. Some, such as the two-man squats,[6] two-man belt exercises,[7] and isometrics[8] are in the realm of beginning exercises since they are taught in the first few weeks of judo training. More complex exercises to increase strength involve specialized push-ups, neck exercises, and weight training.

The advantages of the push-up lie in its

ability to greatly increase existing strength and to tone the muscles. Neck exercises are essential to advanced judo because of the greater use of ne-waza (ground work; see Part II). Weight training is extremely important because it allows you to accomplish a great deal in a relatively short period of time.

There are two ways to approach weight training: (1) use high weight/low repetitions or (2) use low weight/high repetitions. The pros and cons of these methods are argued every month in just about every muscle magazine on the market. The problem is that there are so many different views and opinions that the beginner is often confused and discouraged.

Judo stresses both programs. Program 1, high weight/low reps, is the best method for increasing overall strength and is the key exercise for judo training. This method should be used twice a week. In essence, it means you must lift your maximum weight for a couple of sets of, say, 10 repetitions (20 times, then, in total). Lifting maximum weight 20 times is a tremendous burden. The problem is that the body structure itself cannot take this continual amount of muscular stress, not—and this is the ultimate aim of judo—if you intend to do it the rest of your life in a manner that is beneficial to you rather than destructive.[9]

The solution, then, is to implement Program 2 once a week to supplement the power benefits of Program 1. Program 2, low weight/high repetitions, gives the muscles an aerobic workout as well as the ability to heal themselves. Too often students come to me and tell me of an injury they received doing something that ordinarily would not have injured them. The reason for the injury is that the weight training of Program 1 actually weakens the body's structure temporarily, and even a slight exertion can injure it. However, by doing Program 2 you can strengthen the weakened structure to prevent injury.

For the sake of judo, there is really no need to weight train more than three days a week and this weight training should be preceded and followed by a rigorous 15-minute session of stretching and/or yoga exercises.

Although it is true that weight training does not hinder flexibility to a great extent, judo's need for flexibility is greater than most other sports. Therefore, even a slight hindrance is intolerable. So it is absolutely necessary to stretch after a workout.

An important question asked by many advanced judoka is "If I train extra-hard on the weights, won't the increased strength make up for some minor flaws in my techniques?"

There are two points to the answer. First, muscle strength increases with rest, so it is very important to give your body at least a day of nonweight training between workouts. Most judoka who weight train do so on Monday, Wednesday, and Friday and either judo train in addition to the weights on those days and take Tuesday and Thursday as rest days or judo train only on Tuesday and Thursday and weight train only on Monday, Wednesday, and Friday. The point is that there should be only three days a week of weight training for the active judoka. Remember, you are not a competitive bodybuilder; you are simply using weights to supplement your

strength training. Therefore, split workouts, etc., are not really applicable to judo. Also be sure to do Program 1 on Monday and Friday and Program 2 on Wednesday, as discussed earlier.

The second part of the question raises a sore point with classical judoists. For the *sport-only* judoka, the use of strength often outweighs skill. However for a true judoka, skill with strength is the best combination. I have often competed against open weight competitors (I weigh 140 pounds) and have either held my own or beaten them outright. I rely on skill and mushin rather than strength alone.

SPECIALIZED PUSH-UPS

Leg Elevation Push-Ups

One of the best push-ups for the upper shoulders and upper arms, this push-up involves elevating your legs by putting the balls of your feet on a bench or chair (*photo 3-1*). Lower yourself to the ground (*photo 3-2*) and bring yourself back up again (*photo 3-3*).

Key points: Try to keep your back straight and use the power of your arms *alone* to initiate the up/down action.

Repetitions: Start at 25 and build to 100.

Elevated Dip Push-Ups

For this push-up, use three benches or chairs, one for the legs and one each for the hands (*photo 3-4*). The body is dipped downward beyond the level of the benches (*photo 3-5*) and pushed back up again (*photo 3-6*). Experiment with different hand positions. In this sequence I have positioned them with fingers pointing away from my body, but you should try them at all angles. This is an excellent exercise for the chest and arm muscles.

Repetitions: Start at 25 and build to 100.

Hand Stand Push-Ups

Using the wall as support, bring yourself up into a tripod position (*photo 3-7*), resting your head on the mat. Be sure that you are not too close to or far away from the wall. If you are too far away from it for good balance,

3-1

3-2

3-3

3-4

3-5

3-6

3-7

3-8

3-9

your back will be arched too much; moving too close to the wall, you risk losing your balance from fatigue. Find your own happy medium.

To do the exercise, bring yourself up into a handstand *(photo 3-8)* and back down into tripod position *(photo 3-9)*. This is an excellent exercise for back and shoulder strength.

Repetitions: Start at 15 and build to 100.

NECK EXERCISES

Beginning judoka learn a number of basic exercises to make the neck stronger and more flexible.[10] However, as you begin extensive work on ne-waza (ground work) techniques, you often must rely on the lifting power of your head and neck to get you out from under your opponent. It is therefore necessary to learn to take weight on the head and neck. The following exercises were developed for this purpose.

Elevated Neck Stands

With a partner holding your legs *(photo 3-10)*, rock backward and forward on your neck *(photo 3-11)*.

Note: It is important to have your partner hold your legs up for balance, but you must support *most*, if not *all*, of your weight on your neck. Your partner should not be holding you up. He must, however, always be alert to support your weight by pulling upward should you lose your balance.

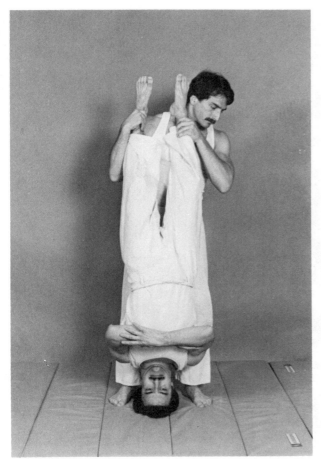

3-10

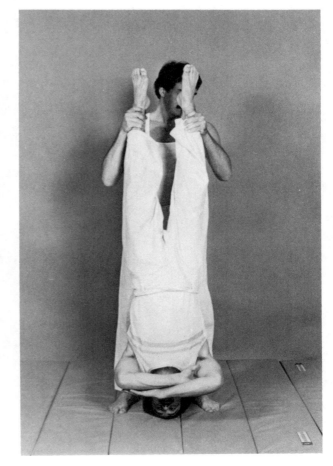

3-11

Rollovers

This is an excellent all-around neck exercise. Begin by placing your head on the mat and grasping your ankles. Your feet should be arm's length away from your head *(photo 3-12)*. Leap into the air by pushing off with your feet, keeping all your weight on your head while retaining a light grip on your legs *(photo 3-13)*. Come back to the mat by placing your feet back on the ground, arching the back and keeping the neck up *(photo 3-14)*.

Note: Be sure the center point of the motion is the top of the head. At no time should the top of the head leave the mat, especially not during the leap-over and recovery.

WEIGHT TRAINING
Barbell Curls

This is a basic biceps development exercise. Take a shoulder-width undergrip and stand erect with barbells across your upper thighs.

Pin your elbows against your sides and move the bar with biceps strength from thighs to chin *(photos 3-15 and 3-16)*. Keep the elbows tight against the body and do not swing the bar to get it started.

Pull-Ups

This is an excellent shoulder and forearm developer. Take a shoulder-width overgrip on the bar *(photo 3-17)* and draw the barbell up to the shoulders *(photo 3-18)*, being sure to keep the bar as close to the body as possible.

Narrow-Grip Pull-Ups

This exercise is done in the same way as the preceding pull-up lift, except the hands grasp the bar in the center *(photo 3-19)* and should actually touch one another. When pulling up *(photo 3-20)*, be sure to keep the bar close to the chest.

3-12

3-13

3-14

3-15

3-16

3-17

3-18

3-19

3-20

Bench Press

Many judoka consider this the best all-around weight exercise for chest strength. To perform it, first remove the bar from the support on the bench *(photo 3-21)* and hold it out above you, bringing your feet down as you lie flat on your back. Hands should be slightly farther apart than shoulder width. Lower the barbell straight down *(photo 3-22)* until it touches the mid-chest, then press it back to arm's length *(photo 3-23)*.

Inclined Bench-Presses

This exercise places stress on the upper pectoral muscles. When you first try this exercise, the barbell will go every way *but* up. Don't worry; this will be corrected after a few sessions.

Note: Start with light weights.

Perform the exercise by taking the barbell off the support and pressing it straight above you at arm's length *(photo 3-24)*. Lower barbell to chest *(photo 3-25)* and then back to a locked-out position *(photo 3-26)*.

Squats

Place the barbells behind your neck and rest it on the back of the neck (or shoulders) *(photo 3-27)*. Keeping the back *straight*, lower your body using the knees *(photo 3-28)* and return to an upright position.

Bent-Over Arm Extensions

Holding a dumbbell in each hand, bend over, allowing the dumbbells to drop directly under the shoulders *(photo 3-29)*. This is the starting position. Draw your arms out, extending the dumbbells to each side *(photo 3-30)*. Return to starting position. This is an excellent exercise to develop upper arm and *shoulder* power.

3-21

3-22

3-23

3-24

3-25

3-26

3-27

3-28

3-29

3-30

Single-Leg Extensions

Tuck one leg under the other and place the top leg in the leg lift section of your lifting bench *(photo 3-31)*. Lift the weights using only the single leg's muscle *(photo 3-32)*. Many experts recommend an isometric contraction at full extension for 10–15 seconds before returning to starting position.

Double-Leg Extension

This is the same as the Single-Leg Extension, except you use both legs *(photos 3-33 and 3-34)*.

Leg Curls

Lie facedown on bench, tucking both feet under the lifting bar *(photo 3-35)* and gripping a part of the bench for support with the hands. Being sure to keep the chest flat on the bench, bring the legs upward toward the buttocks *(photo 3-36)* and then back to starting position. This is an excellent exercise for developing the power necessary to apply *ashiwaza* (leg) techniques.

PURSUING WEIGHT TRAINING

This section on weight training is intended to provide a set of weight exercises that can be applied directly to judo techniques. These particular exercises have been recommended by several competitive judoka. However, this is by no means a complete program of every type of weight exercise available. If you are interested in a more varied program, turn to one of the many fine weight training books available through Contemporary Books, Inc.

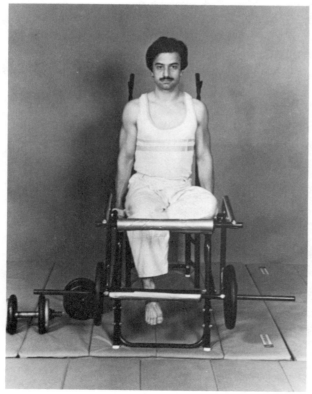

3-31

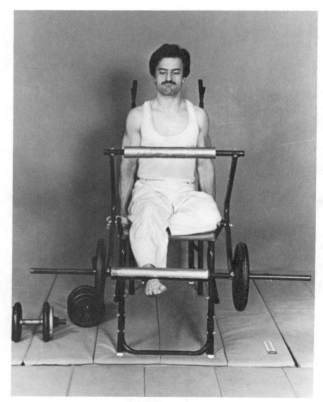

3-32

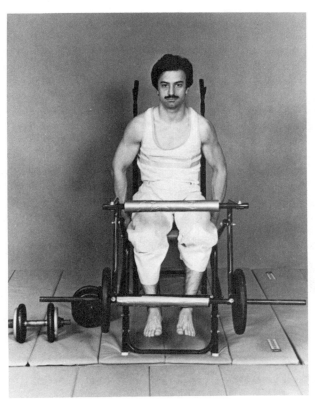

3-33

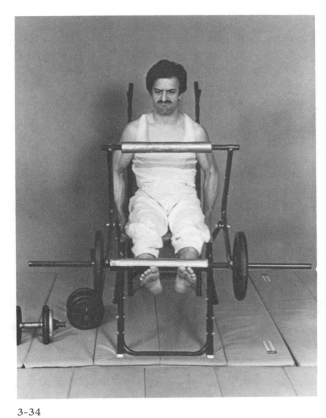

3-34

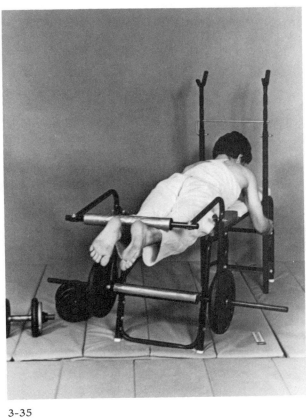

3-35

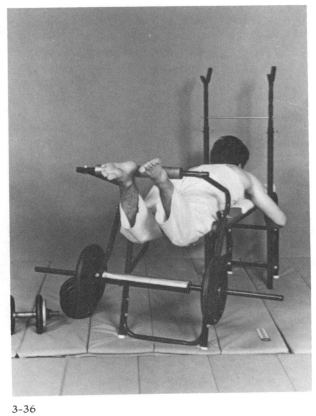

3-36

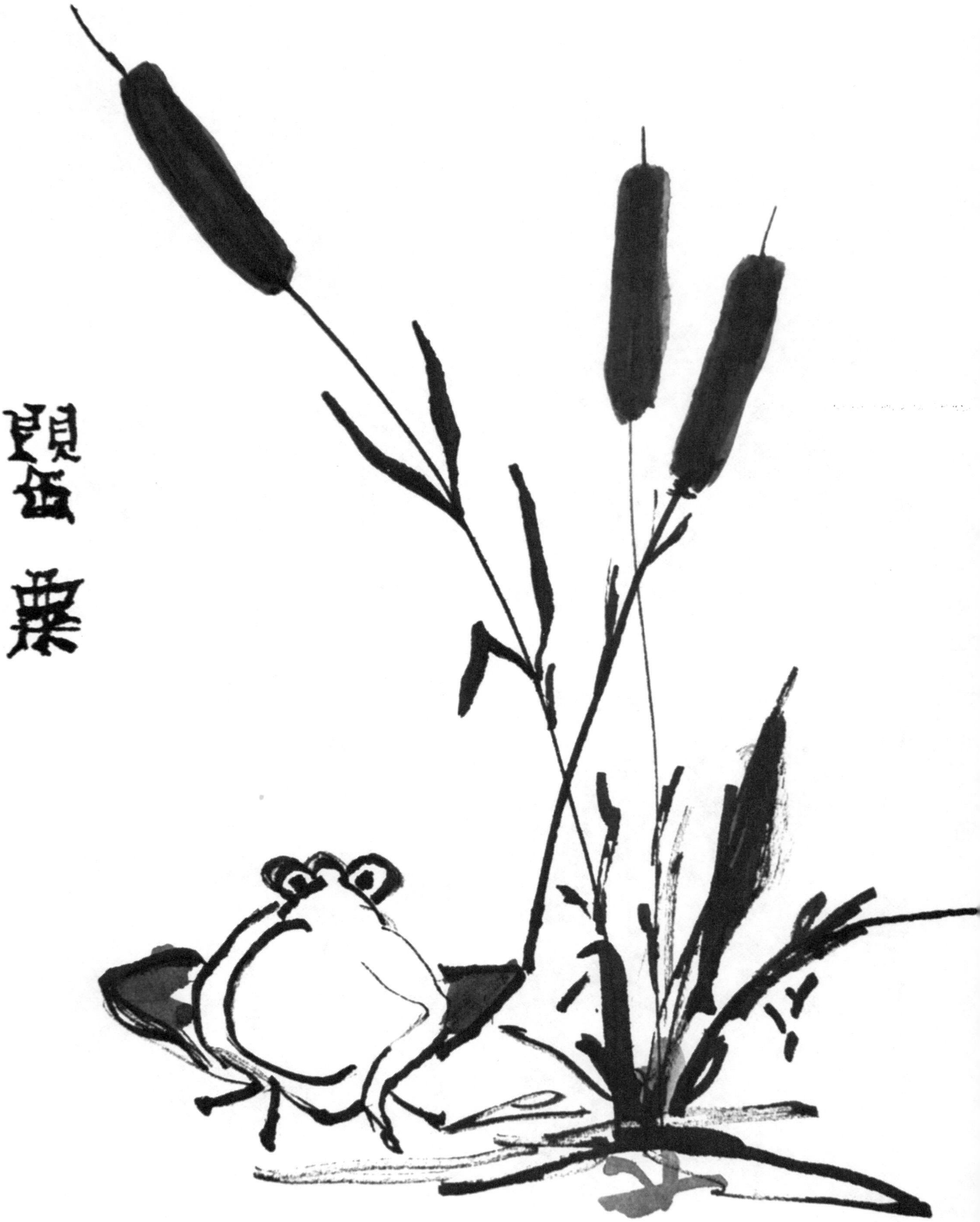

PART II:
THROWING AND LOCKING

The true power of judo lies
In the ability to use
The entire body, not just a single part
During the execution of a technique.
Without *true* power, judo is
Nothing more than a game of
Strength.

Isao Obato

4
ADVANCED THROWING METHODS

Without question, the trademark of judo is the complexity of its many and varied methods of throwing an opponent. Some 97 major judo throws are used in classical judo. Add variations and the lesser known throws, and the count comes close to 250.

The title of this chapter, Advanced Throwing Methods, can be misleading since many of the throws included here appear simple while others appear complex. The main thrust of the judo throwing techniques is found in the *gokyo-waza* throwing system.[11] This system is comprised of the 40 throws taught by the Kodokan. The throws progress from easy to complex. However, there are many variations on these 40 methods as well as lesser known techniques that do not fit into the gokyo-waza categories. This chapter, then, takes a look at the lesser known throws and some of the more complex (advanced) variations on the gokyo-waza system. They are broken down into categories of te-waza (hand throws), koshi-waza (hip throws), ashi-waza (leg throws), and sutemi-waza (sacrificing throws).

Each of the techniques in this chapter contains three steps: *Kuzushi, tsukuri,* and *kake.*

Kuzushi, the first step of a throwing action,[12] is the act of throwing an opponent off balance. Tsukuri, the second phase of throwing,[13] involves moving in for the throw. Kake, the third phase of a throwing action,[14] is the actual execution of the throw.

TE-WAZA (HAND THROWS)

Te-waza are those throws that use the motion of the hands to throw the opponent. This does not mean that other parts of the body don't come into play, for indeed, they often play a very important role. The distinguishing factor in a hand throw is that the controlling actions of the arms set up the throw, off-balance the opponent, and perform the majority of the throwing action.

Te-Guruma (Hand Wheel)

Kuzushi: Face opponent (man on left in photos) at the same time pulling on his right sleeve directly to his right side with your left arm *(photo 4-1)*. At the same time, cross your left foot behind your right foot, pulling your opponent's left leg off the mat *(photo 4-2)*.

Tsukuri: As opponent raises his left foot off the mat, continue to pull him forward as you drop down on your left knee and place the right hand on his right ankle *(photo 4-3)*.

Kake: Continue to pull your opponent to the right and sharply *forward* as you lift his leg off the mat with your right hand *(photo 4-4)*, throwing him completely forward onto his back *(photo 4-5)*.

Ude-Garami-Nage (Arm Entanglement Throw)

Kuzushi: Face opponent (man on left in pho-

tos) and sharply push him to the rear, forcing him to move forward in an opposite reaction *(photo 4-6)*.

Tsukuri: As the opponent steps forward, duck under his armpit, keeping a strong C grip[15] on his *gi* (uniform) *(photo 4-7)* until you have ducked completely under and are at his side *(photo 4-8)*. In this position the opponent is greatly off balance to his front.

Kake: Throw opponent by twisting him clockwise through the grip you have on him, throwing him in a large somersault *(photo 4-9)* onto his back *(photo 4-10)*.

Tip: This is an excellent follow-up throw if your initial seoinage effort fails.

4-1

4-2

4-3

4-4

4-5

4-6

4-7

4-8

4-9

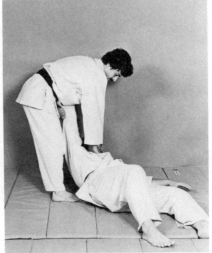

4-10

Morote-Geri (Double Clip)

Kuzushi: Facing opponent (man on left in photos) pull him sharply forward by the sleeves, at the same time ducking under his arms *(photo 4-11)*.

Tsukuri: As you begin your ducking action, reach down and grasp opponent below the knees and above the ankles *(photo 4-12)*. Remember, your initial forward-pulling action will force an instinctive reactionary movement by your opponent and make him pull back.

Kake: As opponent pulls back, sharply lift opponent's legs *(photo 4-13)*, throwing opponent onto his back *(photo 4-14)*.

Kakato-Gaeshi (Heel Overturning)

This technique is also called *te-nage*. Although similar in appearance to the *te-guruma* which throws opponent forward, this technique throws opponent to the side.

Kuzushi: Face opponent (man on left in photos) *(photo 4-15)*. Pull opponent sharply on right sleeve to his right side, at the same time taking a very large step to your left side *(photo 4-16)*. This action will draw the opponent's left foot off the mat.

Tsukuri: Continuing to pull to the opponent's right side, backstep, dropping down on the left knee and placing right hand on opponent's right ankle *(photo 4-17)*. *Note:* Be sure to jerk to the rear as you step back, at the same time pulling on the ankle. This will add greatly to your lifting power.

Kake: Continue the dropping action until you are completely down on your left knee. The instant your knee touches the mat, full effort must be exerted to lift opponent's support foot, pulling his leg off the mat *(photo 4-18)* and throwing him to his right side *(photo 4-19)*.

4-11

4-12

4-13

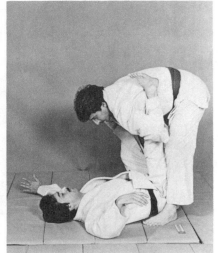

4-14

4-15

4-16

4-17

4-18

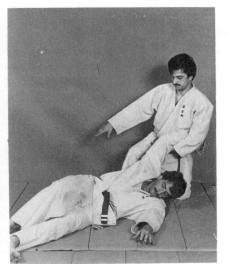

4-19

Eri-Seoinage (Collar Shoulder Throw)

This throw is intended to injure an opponent fatally. It is not intended for competition. It is used when life is threatened. It is a classical throw reminding the judoka of Japan's turbulent history.

Kuzushi: Face opponent (man on left in photos) *(photo 4-20).* Pull opponent off balance to the right front by stepping to the rear.

Tsukuri: Step forward with your right foot and back-pivot with left foot, placing your back to your opponent *(photo 4-21),* at the same time reaching up and under the opponent's right arm and grasping his collar (*eri*) with your right hand while bringing your

right leg between opponent's legs *(photo 4-22 and close-up photo 4-23).*

Kake: To throw opponent, spring upward, at the same time pulling downward *(photo 4-24).* This will lift opponent off his feet. To complete throw, drop down on right knee, slamming opponent's neck and head on the ground (not illustrated). The combined force of his weight and the throw will break his neck. This throw is used only when your life is threatened.

Seoi-Otoshi (Shoulder Drop)

Kuzushi: Facing opponent (man in back in photos), pull him off balance to his right front by pulling his right arm to the side and down *(photo 4-25).*

Tsukuri: Make a three-step *tai-sabaki* (body pivot) by stepping to opponent's right with right foot *(photo 4-26),* bringing the left foot to opponent's left side, and extend the right leg to opponent's right rear, extending the leg to create an obstruction but being sure to keep the knee bent *(photo 4-27).* During the pivot, both arms grasp opponent's right sleeve.

Kake: Pop up, extending the right leg and pulling opponent forward and down by his right arm *(photo 4-28),* which takes him over your leg *(photo 4-29)* and to the ground *(photo 4-30).*

4-20

4-21

4-22

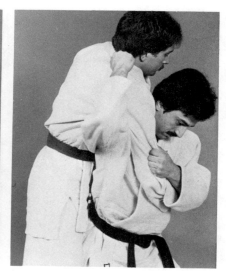

4-23

4-24

4-25

4-26

4-27

4-28

4-29

4-30

Kuki-Nage (Air Throw)

Kuzushi: Facing opponent (man on left in photos), push him hard to the rear to make him react instinctively by pushing forward *(photo 4-31).*

Tsukuri: As opponent moves forward, slip under his right armpit *(photo 4-32)*, ending up on his right side; the opponent will be very off balanced *(photo 4-33)*. Pull up on opponent's right arm (making it straight) with your left arm and place your right hand on opponent's neck *(photo 4-34).*

Kake: To throw opponent, throw your weight forward, at the same time making a clockwise circle with opponent's extended arm and guiding opponent's head as he makes a complete somersault *(photo 4-35)* to the ground *(photo 4-36).*

Hiji-Otoshi (Elbow Drop)

Kuzushi: Facing opponent (man on left in photos) *(photo 4-37)*, put him off balance to his right front by stepping to your right rear with left foot, at the same time bending your right arm and placing the elbow against the side of opponent's head *(photo 4-38).*

Tsukuri: It is important as you backstep in kuzushi to draw opponent's right foot off the mat. In a street situation, the elbow can be slammed against opponent's head, temple, or jaw to incapacitate him further. In contest or practice, the arm is gently placed at the side of the head *(close-up photo 4-39).*

Kake: Throw opponent by twisting hard in a counterclockwise circle, pulling against opponent's head and throwing him into the air *(photo 4-40)* and to the ground *(photo 4-41).*

Note: This is a hand throw, for, although a leg or hip may be used, only the motion of the hands is used to throw the opponent.

4-31

4-32

4-33

4-34

4-35

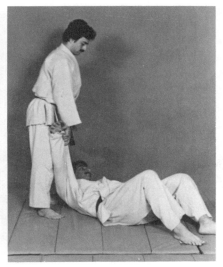

4-36

4-37

4-38

4-39

4-40

4-41

KOSHI-WAZA (HIP THROWS)

In this category of throws, the opponent is thrown over the hip with (1) hip action alone, (2) the aid of the legs with hip power, or (3) the aid of forceful hand motions with hip power.

Yama-Arashi (Mountain Falling)

Kuzushi: Facing opponent (man on right in photos), throw opponent off balance to his left front by pulling him by his left arm *(photo 4-42)*.

Tsukuri: Continue to pull forward as you pivot back to front of opponent *(photo 4-43)*, simultaneously grasping his left arm with both your arms, drawing it across your waist as you begin a lifting action with your left leg *(photo 4-44)*.

Kake: Continue to pull opponent across your waist, at the same time lifting your left leg to sweep opponent off his feet *(photo 4-45)* and to the mat *(photo 4-46)*.

Harai-Makikomi (Sweeping Winding Throw)

Kuzushi: Facing opponent (man on left in photos), pull opponent off balance by pulling his right arm to the right side and sharply downward and forward *(photo 4-47)*.

Tsukuri: Before opponent recovers his balance, wrap his left arm around your waist, grasping it with both hands, while pivoting back to front with opponent. Once you are back to front, begin a lifting action with your right leg *(photo 4-48)*.

Kake: With right leg, continue the lifting action, sweeping opponent off his feet (while leaning into the throw for extra lift and power). This will throw opponent—regardless of size—completely off his feet *(photo 4-49)*. Since you have committed all your weight to this throw in a forward action, you will land on the ground with opponent, safely at his side *(photo 4-50)*.

Note: In a street situation, you can slam your weight downward, adding to the force of the impact on opponent's chest.

4-42

4-43

4-44

4-45

4-46

4-47

4-48

4-49

4-50

O-Tsuri-Goshi (Major Lifting Hip Throw)

This is an excellent throw for a larger man to apply to a shorter, stockier individual.

Kuzushi: Facing opponent (man on left in photos) *(photo 4-51)*, pull him off balance by pulling downward and forward on his left sleeve while bringing your left foot to opponent's left leg *(photo 4-52)*.

Tsukuri: Pivot in a counterclockwise circle on the ball of the left foot, throwing your hip into opponent's midsection while reaching over opponent's shoulder and grasping his belt *(photo 4-53)*.

Kake: To throw opponent, bend down and pop up on knees while simultaneously lifting up on opponent's belt. This will throw opponent into air *(photo 4-54)* and to the ground *(photo 4-55)*.

Seoi-Hane-Goshi (Shoulder Lifting Spring Hip Throw)

Kuzushi: Facing opponent (man on left in photos), push him sharply to the rear while advancing on him in a very aggressive manner *(photo 4-56)*. Instinctive reactionary force will force him to push momentarily against your aggressive advance.

Tsukuri: Timing his resistive push by feeling when he comes forward, leap into the air *(photo 4-57)*, slamming your back into opponent's chest while simultaneously bringing your right elbow under opponent's right armpit and your right leg (bent) just under opponent's right knee *(photo 4-58)*.

Kake: With the force of your leaping body, lift up on your leg (with spring action) while pulling opponent over and down, taking him into the air *(photo 4-59)* and to the mat *(photo 4-60)*.

Tip: The throw works best when kuzushi, tsukuri, and kake are all one fast action.

4-51

4-52

4-53

4-54

4-55

4-56

4-57

4-58

4-59

4-60

Uchi-Makikomi (Inner Winding Throw)

Kuzushi: Facing opponent (man on left in photos), pull him off balance to his right front by yanking to the side and down on opponent's right sleeve *(photo 4-61).*

Tsukuri: Pivot back to front, drawing opponent's right arm across the front of your chest *(photo 4-62)* while slipping your right leg in between opponent's legs *(photo 4-63).*

Kake: To throw opponent, sweep the inner upper thigh of opponent's left leg, at the same time throwing all your weight forward, taking him into the air *(photo 4-64)* and to the ground *(photo 4-65).* Since you have committed all your weight forward to add more power to the throw, you will land safely at opponent's side.

Note: In a street situation, you can cause severe body damage to an opponent by driving your body into his as you both go down. The added weight could break his ribs.

4-61

4-62

4-63

4-64

4-65

ASHI-WAZA (LEG TECHNIQUES)

For this category of throws, you use the action of the legs, coupled with body movements, to throw an opponent to the ground. Ashi-waza take a great deal of timing and leg power, so they are often a tool of experienced judoka.

Kani-Basami (Leg Scissors)

Kuzushi: Facing opponent (man on right in photos) *(photo 4-66)*, pull him sharply downward by the right sleeve (with a slight motion to his rear), at the same time lowering your weight *(photo 4-67)*.

Tsukuri: With the opponent off balance to the rear, place your right hand on the mat, holding opponent's right sleeve with left hand and placing your left leg across opponent's upper thighs and your right leg behind opponent's ankles *(photo 4-68)*.

Kake: Throw opponent by pulling down with the left arm and twisting your lower body and legs in a counterclockwise circle, knocking opponent to the ground *(photo 4-69)*.

Kuchiji-Taoshi (Dead Tree Dropping Throw)

Kuzushi: Facing opponent (man on right in photos) *(photo 4-70)*, push him to the rear as you place your left foot on opponent's left ankle (this action is called *ko-uchi-geri*[17]) *(photo 4-71)*.

Tsukuri: Lift the opponent's left leg up to your right hand, grasping it, at the same time shuffling your left leg *(photo 4-72)* behind opponent's right leg *(photo 4-73)*.

Kake: Sweep opponent's supporting leg out from under him *(photo 4-74)*, taking him to the mat *(photo 4-75)*.

4-66   4-67   4-68   4-69

4-70

4-71

4-72

4-73

4-74

4-75

SUTEMI-WAZA (SACRIFICING THROWS)

These throws sacrifice your own balance in order to throw an opponent to the ground. They are done by falling on either your back (*ma-sutemi*) or your side (*yoko sutemi*).

Tawara-Gaeshi (Bale Throw)

Kuzushi: Facing opponent (man on left in photos) in a deep defensive (*jigotai*) posture, step to rear with left foot, drawing him off balance forward (*photo 4-76*).

Tsukuri: Taking advantage of his off balance position, reach over opponent, grasping him in a bear hug over his upper chest, locking your arms by grasping your right wrist with the left hand (*photo 4-77*).

Kake: Fall to the rear, pulling opponent down with you in a somersault (*photo 4-78*), forcing him to fall near your upper shoulder (*photo 4-79*).

Hiji-Otoshi (Dead Elbow Drop)

Kuzushi: Facing opponent (man on left in photos) (*photo 4-80*), step to rear with left foot, pulling hard on opponent's right sleeve, forcing him to shift his weight forward (*photo 4-81*).

Tsukuri: Turn opponent's arm so his elbow is facing the sky, at the same time placing his arm under your left armpit, bringing your arm across his elbow, and resting your hand on his inner upper right thigh (*photo 4-82*).

Kake: Bring all your weight to bear on his elbow, forcing opponent face first into the mat (*photo 4-83*). Maintain position with pressure on opponent's elbow.

4-76

4-77

4-78

4-79

4-80

4-81

4-82

4-83

5
HOLDS, LOCKS, AND NE-WAZA STRATEGY

Holds, locks, and ne-waza (ground work) strategy fall into the category referred to in judo as *katame-waza*, or grappling techniques. Grappling is necessarily a short-range technique; unlike striking (see Part IV), which can be initiated at up to six feet, grappling involves very close contact. Basically, grappling involves holds, locks, chokes, and escapes.

Holds are used primarily after a throw or when a throw fails. In competition, where holds (*osaekomi-waza*) are used primarily, you achieve a full point if you hold your opponent on his back for 30 seconds. However, for practical street combat, hold-downs are of little value. The reason for this is that they afford the opportunity for your opponent to bite, pinch, claw, and gouge to get out. Naturally, in competition, such actions are prohibited.

Locking techniques (*kansetsu-waza*), however, afford true control in both competition and self-defense. The problem with them practically speaking, is that they are difficult to apply against a larger, stronger opponent. Only expert skill and timing can overcome a

stronger man with these techniques. The slightest error or misjudgment in timing can mean your life in certain situations. The complete art of judo has a lock for just about every joint in the body (most are prohibited in competition—except those applied against the elbow). Perhaps the most common of the locking methods are those applied by hyperextending the elbow joint. The wrist joint can be manipulated five different ways (prohibited in sport play), the outward twist being the most common. The shoulder is also often a target, either using the leverage of the straight arm or by bending the arm at right angles and cracking it.

Choking techniques (*shime-waza*) are important supplementary techniques, unique in that they can easily produce controlled unconciousness with little or no risk (when correctly applied). They are an integral part of judo ground work, where they reach a high degree of technical sophistication. There are actually three different categories of choking methods.

The choke is applied by pressure on the

windpipe, cutting off the supply of air. It is unpleasant to experience, dangerous (as the cartilage of the windpipe could be crushed) and produces unconsciousness in about 60 seconds, from which recovery is spontaneous if the hold is not continued past the point of unconsciousness.

Arterial strangle applies pressure to the carotid arteries on either side of the neck, which carry blood to the brain. When both arteries are compressed long enough (about 5–15 seconds) unconsciousness comes swiftly. If the hold is stopped at the point of unconsciousness, recovery of consciousnees is usually (but not always) spontaneous. It is wise to apply *kappo* (a special first aid) to such victims. When correctly applied, there is absolutely no discomfort. In fact, many find it to be a stimulating and relaxing experience.

A cautionary note is indicated here. Cutting off the blood supply to the brain to the point of unconsciousness is safe if done *infrequently*. But too often, competitors, hoping they can break the hold, choose to struggle on rather than giving up when control is obvious. This is foolish.

In the nerve strangle, pressure is applied against one or both sides of the neck against one or more nerve ganglia. This induces, via the vagus nerve, a reflex stoppage of the heart and massive loss of blood pressure; unconsciousness is instantaneous. Recovery is *not* spontaneous since the heart nerves have received huge inhibitory stimulus; they may need to be artificially restimulated through *kappo*. The best method involves firm and precise, 45-degree upward blows with the heel of the hand in the region of the the sixth thoracic vertebra (at the bottom of the shoulder blades).

This chapter will deal with both sport and self-defense applications of katame-waza. Since most of the major holds, chokes, and elbow locks were detailed in my first book, *The Complete Book of Judo*, we will deal mainly with (1) *kote-waza*, wrist locks for self-defense control; (2) *ashi-kansetsu-waza*, leg locking methods for self-defense control; (3) ne-waza (ground work) strategy for pinning an unwilling opponent in judo competition; and (4) *kaeshi-waza*, countering methods to certain

commonly applied hold-downs in competition.

KOTE-WAZA (WRIST LOCKS)

Although the arts of aikido and aiki-jujutsu primarily use pressure on the wrist to execute control and throwing techniques, judo uses a wide variety of wrist manipulations to control the opponent, to take the fight out of him (such as a come-along hold), and to break the joint to incapacitate the opponent. We will examine four popular methods of kote-waza.

Renkoho-Gaeshi (Arm/Wrist Come-Along)

This is an excellent holding technique to take someone forcibly without his consent. It is useful for police who want to place a suspect in a vehicle as well as for removing a drunk from a bar (when hitting him is not possible; for example, if the drunk is your uncle).

The hold is effected by applying reverse

5-1

pressure against the finger joints, at the same time hyperextending the elbow and applying pressure against it. Finger pressure is applied upward, in the direction of the opponent's shoulder, while elbow pressure is applied forward, in the direction you plan to take the opponent *(photo 5-1)*.

Gyaku-Kote-Gaeshi (Reverse Wrist Turning Lock)

Again, this lock makes an excellent come-along technique. It can also be used to pin someone to the ground or break his wrist. The result is determined by the amount of pressure exerted on the wrist. Slight pressure can be used to direct the opponent to go where you want him to. Medium pressure directed straight down will force the opponent to his knees and immobilize him. If he attempts to resist, extreme pressure will snap the wrist. Pain from a broken wrist is severe and will immobilize your opponent completely.

To apply lock, stand first with hands extended as if the two of you were about to shake hands (opponent will be extending his right hand). Grasp his hand with your right hand and turn it clockwise so that the elbow points upward to the sky. Hold the opponent's hand with both of your hands, placing your fingers in the palm and the thumb on the back of the hand. Pressure is applied with a slight clockwise twist with a sharp pressure toward opponent's elbow *(photo 5-2)*.

Kote-Gaeshi (Wrist Turning Lock)

This is perhaps the most useful and versatile wrist lock in martial arts. This lock can be used to snap the wrist or throw the opponent to the ground. Again, these actions are determined by the amount of pressure exerted on the wrist. A very sharp and powerful twist will separate the wrist, breaking it in half. However, even pressure exerted straight down on the wrist will force the opponent to fall. This type of pressure cannot be resisted. If the opponent tries to resist, he will find himself with a broken wrist.

To apply this lock, have your partner extend his right hand. Place both thumbs against the back of the hand; the fingers will grasp the palm. Your grip should be viselike. Turn the wrist counterclockwise, allowing for a slight bend at the elbow joint *(photo 5-3)*.

Tesubi-Gaeshi (Bent-Arm Twist)

Also called *sankyu*, this is a very effective come-along restraint technique as well as a way to dislocate an opponent's wrist.

To apply hold, have your partner extend his right arm as if shaking your hand. Grasp his fingers with your hand, as if you were shaking his hand, and grasp his wrist with your left hand. Retaining your grip, duck under his armpit in a counterclockwise rotation, ending up at his side. Bend his elbow and apply pressure by twisting the arm counterclockwise. To prevent opponent from slipping out of your hold, be sure to keep his elbow bent and facing the sky *(photo 5-4)*.

ASHI-KANSETSU-WAZA (LEG LOCKING TECHNIQUES) WITH SEKIZUKI-WAZA (BACK LOCKING)

The leg locks, prohibited in competition (except for one noted later in the book), are excellent ways to pin and immobilize an attacker. They are especially useful after the use of atemi-waza (striking) and nage-waza (throwing) techniques.

Ashi-Hishigi (Front-Leg Entanglement)

A very effective and painful method of pinning and incapacitating your opponent. Severe pressure in this leg lock can break the opponent's knee.

You have just knocked your opponent to his back *(photo 5-5)* and are standing over him, holding his left foot in your left hand. Place your left foot next to opponent's left hip, putting the opponent's instep on your left side *(photo 5-6)*. To apply pressure, simply lean your weight forward *(photo 5-7)*.

5-2

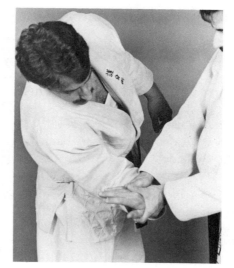

5-3

5-4

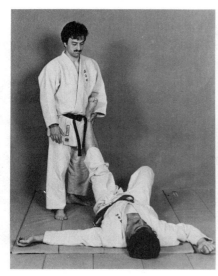

5-5

5-6

5-7

Ebi-Garami (Lobster Entanglement)

Perhaps the most effective of the leg locks to immobilize an opponent for a long period of time.

Begin by standing over your opponent (right in photos), whom you have just knocked to the ground on his face *(photo 5-8)*. *Note:* If you have knocked him on his back and want to apply this lock, simply grab his leg firmly and twist him over.

You should be holding his right leg with your left hand. Place your left leg to the side and around the opponent's bent leg, leaning your weight forward as if to trap your left shinbone in the *V* of opponent's bent leg. Pressure is exerted by leaning forward. In reality, this leaning action forces your shinbone to pinch the nerves in opponent's calf and upper thigh *(photos 5-9 and 5-10)*.

For added immobilization, you can also lock the opponent's elbow and wrist *(photo 5-11)*.

Ashi-Garami with Ude-Hishigi-Gatame (Leg Entanglement with Arm Lock)

This method of locking the leg is actually a method of gaining better control over an opponent and does not inflict a great deal of pain on the leg itself. Because of this, this hold is legal (and perhaps is only useful) in competition.

You have been knocked down on your back, and your opponent (right in photos) is advancing on you. Place your left leg under his right leg and grasp his right sleeve with your left hand *(photo 5-12)*. Circle your left leg clockwise around the opponent's right leg, trapping his leg *(photo 5-13)*. Pin his knee to the mat with your entangling leg *(photo 5-14)* and secure a *ude-gatame* (arm lock) on opponent's right elbow *(photo 5-15)*.

Gyaku-Sekizuki-Getsu (Reverse Back Lock)

This hold, which is prohibited in competition, has very little practical use other than its ability to snap opponent's back or hold attacker until help arrives.

The hold is executed by first throwing an opponent to his back, grasping his legs, and turning him over. Stand at approximately the opponent's waist and grasp both his legs firmly *(photo 5-16)*. Tuck his legs up under your armpits and arch the opponent's body, using your arms for support and your entire body for power *(photo 5-17)*. To put pressure on opponent, lean backward while forcing the opponent to arch. *Note:* Arching pressure applied with a quick and powerful jerking action can cause severe damage to opponent's spine. Techniques like this are used only when your life is threatened.

5-8

5-9

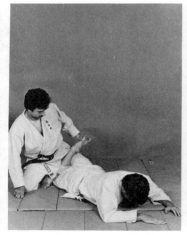

5-10

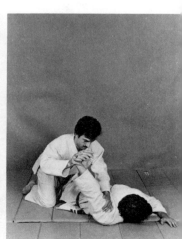

5-11

5-12

5-13

5-14

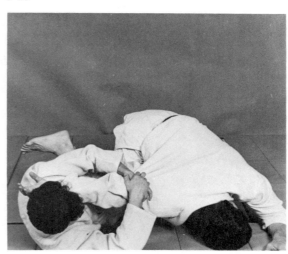

5-15

5-16

5-17

NE-WAZA STRATEGY

One of the questions I am asked most frequently by progressing judoka is "Does judo teach how to get in and out of hold-downs?" What they are asking, quite simply, is if there is any such thing as ne-waza (ground work) strategy.

Ne-waza strategy is defined as the ability to control your opponent to get him from a kneeling position to a hold-down. Of course, you can expend a great amount of energy attempting to wrestle the opponent to the mat, or you can use "maximum efficiency with the least effort" and strategically get the opponent into a pin. Ne-waza strategy is for sport use only since it is rare that the right circumstances will occur on the street. In order to use such strategy, you must first have a working knowledge of the holding techniques that are to be applied.[18]

Kesa-Gatame
(Bent-Arm Drag)

You and your opponent have lost your balance and have both fallen to the mat. Your wish is to secure your opponent with a *kesa-gatame* (scarf hold) technique. To accomplish this, you shuffle in close to opponent (left in photos) *(photo 5-51)* and wrap your left arm around opponent's right arm, trapping it in a V position behind opponent's back, at the same time pressing opponent's head to the mat with right hand *(photo 5-19)*. Roll him over in a somersault by continuing to press his head down and forcing him to roll over through the adverses pressure on opponent's trapped right arm *(photo 5-20)*. Now that the opponent is on his back, pin him with *kesa-gatame*[19] *(photo 5-21)*.

Kami-Shiho-Gatame
(Chin Spin)

Again, both you and your opponent have lost your balance and have fallen to a kneeling position on the mat *(photo 5-22)*. Your desire is to pin opponent on his back with a *kami-shiho-gatame* (upper four quarters hold). To accomplish this, grasp your opponent's (left in photos) chin with both hands and spin yourself in a counterclockwise circle onto the mat *(photo 5-23)*. This twists the opponent's head, which forces him to fall to his back on the mat *(photo 5-24)*. Before your opponent can protect himself in a more defensive posture, pin his shoulders with a *kami-shiho-gatame*[20] *(photo 5-25)*.

5-18

5-19

5-20

5-21

5-22

5-23

5-24

5-25

5-26

5-27

5-28

5-29

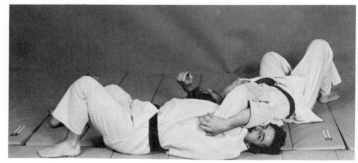

5-30

5-31

Yoko-Shiho-Gatame (Bale Throw with Pin)

You and your opponent have lost your balance and are kneeling and facing each other on the mat *(photo 5-26)*. Your desire is to pin your opponent (left in photos) in a *yoko-shiho-gatame* (side quarters hold). To accomplish this, reach both your arms under opponent's arms, placing both your hands in the middle of his back *(photo 5-27)*. Roll backward *(photo 5-28)*; the adverse pressure on opponent's shoulders will force him to roll with you in a large somersault *(photo 5-29)*, making him land on his back *(photo 5-30)*. Before he can get control of you, secure a *yoko-shiho-gatame*[21] *(photo 5-31)*.

Morote-Ude-Gatame (Double Arm Lock against Protective Squat)

In this case, your opponent (left in photos) has gone down on all fours in an effort to prevent you from applying katame-waza on him. This is a very common protective position in judo *(photo 5-32)*. Your desire is to apply a *morote-ude-gatame* (double-arm lock) on him. To accomplish this, kneel at opponent's side, grasping his right arm with both your hands while trapping his left arm with your legs *(photo 5-33)*. Carefully pull him to the mat *(photo 5-34)* and apply pressure to his right elbow/shoulder with both arms (pulling away from him and in toward you)*(photo 5-35)*.

5-32

5-33

5-34

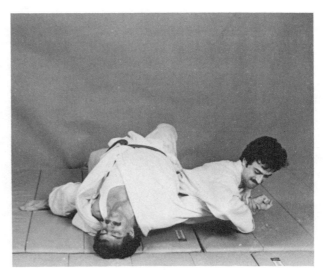

5-35

Arm Lift into Ude-Gatame (Arm Lock against Protective Squat)

Again, your opponent (left in photos) attempts to prevent ne-waza (ground work) by squatting on all fours *(photo 5-36)*. Kneel at his side, reaching under him and grasping his right arm with your left hand, at the same time pulling upward on his arm and driving his shoulder to the mat with the pressing weight of your body *(photo 5-37)*. Push downward on the opponent, at the same time pulling up until he is on his back *(photo 5-38)*. Working *very quickly*, tuck the opponent's right arm under your left armpit as you move on your left side *(photo 5-39)*. Be sure to place your right hand on opponent's head to help control him as you position yourself on your side.

Tuck your left shin (your leg is bent) at opponent's right side, placing your right leg on opponent's midsection to prevent him from rolling out of hold (the right leg maintains a constant downward pressure on opponent's abdomen). Clasp your hands together and apply pressure, hyperextending the elbow by leaning back *(photo 5-40)*.

5-36

5-37

5-38

5-39

5-40

Juji-Gatame (Cross-Arm Lock against Sitting Squat)

Opponent (left in photos) has gone down on all fours and is sitting on his heels to prevent ne-waza. Your recourse is to stand at his side *(photo 5-41)*, grasping his right arm, with both hands yanking it free from its protective position *(photo 5-42)*.

With a tight grip, *fall* into a juji-gatame.[22] *Note:* In order to turn the opponent on to his back, you must retain a very tight grip on the arm you intend to lock (in this case, his right arm) and literally fall to the mat in order to create enough force to turn him *(photo 5-43)*.

Kata-Ha-Jime (Wing Choke against Sitting Squat)

Again, your opponent (left in photos) has gone down on all fours to prevent ne-waza play. In addition, he has sat on his heels and covered his head *(photo 5-44)*.

Standing over him, reach to his right side with your right hand grasping the left lapel (eri) of his gi *(photo 5-45)*. Fall onto your left side, spinning clockwise while retaining your lapel grip. This will force opponent to roll over you onto his back. Reach your left arm under his armpit and secure a *kata-ha-jime*[23] choking technique *(photo 5-46)*.

5-41

5-42

5-43

5-44

5-45

5-46

KAESHI-WAZA (COUNTERING TECHNIQUES)

Sometimes your opponent is too swift for you, and he begins to secure a hold-down or choking technique before you can prevent it. *Kaeshi-waza*, the art of turning the tables, will allow you to escape such a hold. The idea behind *kaeshi-waza* is to effect it *before* the opponent has fully secured his hold-down.

Counter to Kesa-Gatame (Scarf Hold)

Opponent (left in photos) has begun to secure a kesa-gatame[19] hold *(photo 5-47)*. Reach around with your right arm grasping his belt, at the same time grasping his belt with your left hand. Move in as close as possible to opponent's side while rolling up on your own right side *(photo 5-48)*. With a pow-erful lifting and turning action, throw your weight onto your left side, at the same time pulling the opponent around you *(photo 5-49)* and safely to the mat *(photo 5-50)*. You may now apply a hold-down of your own.

Counter to Kata-Gatame (Shoulder Hold)

Opponent (front in photos) has begun to secure a kata-gatame[24] on you *(photo 5-51)*. Straighten your trapped right arm, placing it on the back of opponent's neck and driving his head to the mat *(photo 50-52)*. Continue to drive his head toward his waist while rolling him over using your left arm *(photo 5-53)*, forcing him to land on his back *(photo 5-54)*. Before he can recover, pin him with kami-shiho-gatame[20] *(photo 5-55)*.

5-47

5-48

5-49

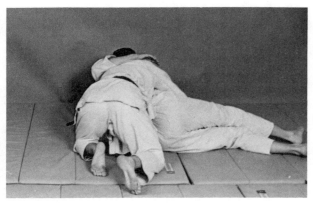

5-50

5-51

5-52

5-53

5-54

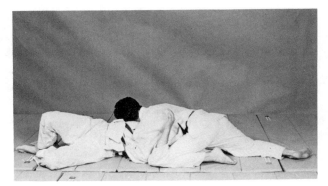

5-55

Counter to Kami-Shiho Gatame (Upper Four Corners Hold)

Opponent (on top in photos) has begun to secure a *kami-shiho gatame*[20] *(photo 5-56)* on you. Before his grip is secure, press his chest upward while rolling over, placing your feet on his shoulders *(photo 5-57)*. Using feet and hands, push yourself free *(photo 5-58)*. Before opponent can move into a defensive position, grasp his right arm in your left hand, placing your right hand at the base of his skull *(photo 5-59)*. Using the arm as a lever and the pressing motion on his neck, roll opponent over onto his back *(photo 5-60)*, securing your own *kami-shiho gatame (photo 5-61)*.

Counter to Gyaku-Juji-Jime (Reverse Cross-Choke)

Opponent (on top in photos) has secured a tight *gyaku-juji-jime*[25] and has begun to choke you *(photo 5-62)*. Grasp opponent's right wrist with your right hand while placing your left forearm on the back of his elbow *(photo 5-63)*. Using your weight and arm strength, knock opponent off you by putting pressure on his hyperextended elbow joint *(photo 5-64)*. Keeping opponent's face in the mat, secure a *waki-gatame* (armpit hold)[26] on him *(photo 5-65)*.

5-56

5-57

5-58

5-59

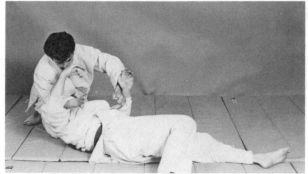

5-60

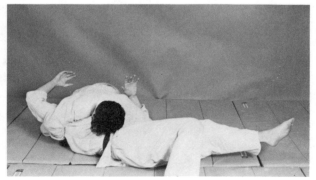

5-61

5-62

5-63

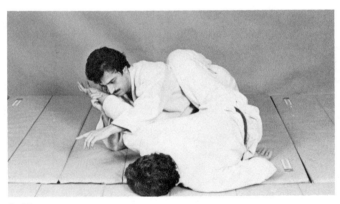

5-64

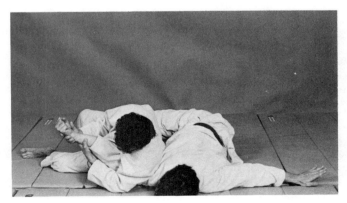

5-65

PART III: THE FORMAL EXERCISES OF JUDO (KATA)

Kata is the heart, soul and
Breath of true judo, the
Gentle Way.
Without the kata, judo is
Nothing more than
Japanese wrestling.

6
WHAT ARE KATA?

Like most forms of budo, the practice of judo involves the perfection of kata. Kata are graduated exercises of prearranged movements. They include all the forms of throwing, grappling, and striking/kicking the vital points, together with the cutting and thrusting with the dagger and sword. These prearranged techniques are performed by two people (with one exception). The performer is called the *tori* and the partner is called the *uke*.

Both tori and uke must execute and demonstrate the movements with complete energy of mind and body to comply with the great ideal of judo: "maximum employment of one's capacities directed to a fixed purpose through the application of the techniques of judo."

The kata stress four points:

1. The optimum employment of energy, or *seiryoku zenyo* (maximum efficiency with least effort).
2. The kata is teamwork between a tori and an uke. It thus conforms to the judo concept of *jita kyoei*,[27] or mutual benefit

and welfare.
3. Kata stress the concept of *ju*, or the ability to give way in order to overcome an opponent.
4. A kata teaches one to apply the concept of mushin (see Chapter 2) since all kata should be done in an empty (but alert/tranquil) relaxed state.

However, not all kata are intended solely for the purpose of teaching. Some, such as the *Koshiki-no-kata* (Forms of Antiquity) not only teach but also preserve the ancient concepts and techniques of Kito-ryu jujutsu.

Aside from preserving and teaching, kata practice is an exercise in stylistic movement, of which it may be said that the practice resembles the quasi-religious character of Shinto dance ritual both in the past as well as in the present. Kata set off the beauty of human body gestures and illustrate the performers' physical and spiritual mastery.

The kata is therefore a tool not only for the physical mastery of the body (techniques) but also a tool for the discipline of the mind and the union of mind and body (with the incorporation of the Zen principles found in Chapter 2). It is through the kata that true appreciation of judo as a way of life is realized. Kata allows judo to rise above mere sport and allows it to enter the realm of martial *art* and spiritual conditioning.

There are nine main kata taught through the Kodokan, along with several minor ones. The nine kata are listed below in the order they are to be learned; the lesser kata are taught at the instructor's discretion.

1. Nage-no-kata (forms of throwing)
2. Katame-no-kata (forms of holding)
Both kata 1 and 2 are called Randori-no-kata
3. Gonosen-no-kata (forms of throws and counterthrows)
4. Kime-no-kata (forms of self-defense)
5. Itsutsu-no-kata (forms of five)
6. Ju-no-kata (forms of gentleness)
7. Koshiki-no-kata (forms of antiquity)
8. Kodokan Goshin-jutsu (Kodokan self-defense techniques)
9. Joshi Judo-goshin-ho (Kodokan self-defense for women)

Of lesser importance, but still in use today, is the *Seiryoku-zenyo-kokumin-taiiku*, an exercise series aimed at developing all muscles of the body in proper harmony and increasing harmonious strength. It is a one-man kata consisting of 28 individual exercises in the use of *tai-sabaki* (body movement) and atemi-waza (striking/kicking). The kata was produced in 1880, and many of its techniques are outdated.

The *Renkoho-no-kata*, or forms of arrest, is a very short kata illustrating the concept of control. It is a useful kata for police for it allows one to forcibly move an opponent from one place to another.

The *Kime-shiki*, or forms of decision, is an exercise to build up the body's reflexes and develop fast graceful movements. The kata consists of five techniques kneeling (*idori*) and five techniques standing (*tachiai*).

In addition to these there are *Shobu-no-kata*, or forms of attack (or contest), and *Go-no-kata*, or forms of force. The latter is more like a kata of karate-do than of judo, since it is a prearranged pattern of blocks, strikes, and kicks done with power and focus (*kime*).

THE NINE MAIN KATA
NAGE-NO-KATA

The *Nage-no-kata*, or forms of throwing, is the first judo kata and consists of 15 throws divided into five sets of three techniques each. These techniques were selected as the ideal model to aid the study of the theory of the various throwing categories. It was invented by Dr. Kano, who incorporated his *ji* (see Chapter 2) into its movements.

Nage-no-kata teaches three very important principles: (1) attack and defense; (2) *shintai*, displacement of opponent's energy; and (3) tai-sabaki, body movements and weight shifting. Tradition demands that the Nage-no-kata be performed at all judo demonstrations and competitions to illustrate the key factors in throwing.

KATAME-NO-KATA

This second judo kata, the forms of grappling, consists of 15 techniques from the art of grappling. The kata is divided into holding, locking, and choking methods. The five techniques in each of these categories were selected as the most pertinent examples to explain the theory and practice of effective grappling.

The kata was designed by Dr. Kano in the first part of the 20th century. This kata along with the Nage-no-kata, make up the series of movements called Randori-no-kata (forms of contest), since these techniques are most often used in competitive judo.

GONOSEN-NO-KATA

Many claim that the forms of throwing and counterthrowing, the third kata of judo, make up the third and last segment of the *Randori-no-kata*, that is, the representative techniques used in competition. To perform it, the uke attempts a given throw while the tori responds with a prearranged counterthrow. The kata was created in 1917 by judo masters from the Waseda University in Japan.

KIME-NO-KATA

Called the forms of self-defense, *Kime-no-kata* is the fourth kata of judo. It is divided into two sets of 8 and 12 moves respectively. The first series, idori, is performed in a kneeling position; the second series, tachiai, is performed standing. The kata is also called *Shinken-shobu-no-kata*, or forms of combat.

It constitutes the simplest and most efficacious methods of defense against attacks from bare hands, daggers, and swords. Its proper execution demands great attention and should be practiced slowly at first so you learn the fine points of its execution. Remember that the spirit of this kata lies in its combat essence.

The understanding and the execution of this kata teach you the principles of general judo, expecially those of strangulation (*shimewaza*), body locks, and striking/kicking.

Kime-no-kata must be done in a set tempo/rhythm:

1. The tori *and* uke must pause a few seconds before each sequence so as to bring full concentration to the moment at hand.
2. Uke *always* attacks in a rapid, *violent* manner.
3. Deflect/defense must be even more rapid by tori, who should hold uke under complete control for several seconds. Uke then signals surrender by tapping tori twice on the body. However, when the sequence ends in a throw or an atemi (strike) there is no sign of surrender by uke.

ITSUTSU-NO-KATA

This is the fifth judo kata and the first of the *complex* kata. It represented for its founder, Dr. Kano, the heart of judo (however, Dr. Kano did not name the kata).

It constitutes the synthesis of all fundamental forms of body movement and illustrates the correspondence/communion of these five basic judo principles with the principles of the universe. It is based, some believe, on the Taoist principle of the microcosm (body) corresponding to the macrocosm (universe) in every detail. Since the Japanese borrowed many beliefs from the Chinese, it is wise to assume that *Itsutsu-no-kata* is based on Chinese Taoist principles.

Because of its high philosophical stature, this kata must be done with style and majesty and must flow smoothly *without* any hesitation.

The five principles of *Itsutsu-no-kata* are listed below.

1. Concentration of energy and action. *Technique:* direct push.
2. Reaction and nonresistance. *Technique:* evasion.
3. Cyclic principle of the circle or the whirlwind. *Technique:* centrifugal force.
4. Alternation of the pendulum. *Technique:* flux and reflux.
5. Principle of void. *Technique:* inertia.

JU-NO-KATA

The forms of gentleness comprise the sixth kata of judo and the second of the complex kata. It is composed of 15 techniques in three sets of five.

The Ju-no-kata techniques are comprised of gentle movements designed to teach the body control when attacking or defending and also how to employ one's strength most effectively. In the days when women were not allowed to compete in competitions, the Ju-no-kata was considered their special province. It is also favored by elders of advanced rank.

KOSHIKI-NO-KATA

Koshiki-no-kata (forms of antiquity)—a favorite of this author—represents the seventh kata in judo and the third of the so-called complex or superior kata. It originated from the Kito-ryu style of jujutsu (see Chapter 1). Dr. Kano invented this pattern as a way of preserving the most representative techniques from judo's heritage.

For Dr. Kano, Kime-no-kata constituted preparatory training for real combat, Itsutsu-no-kata represented synthesis of the macrocosm/microcosm, and Koshiki-no-kata was the sum of these principles defined by tradition and experience through the ages and expressed by the image of combat itself.

That is why Dr. Kano considered this kata the truest, most vital approach to real fighting, and that is why this kata is the most supreme (complex) of them all and should be performed only by *dan* level judoka.

It is comprised of throws, most of which are sutemi (sacrificing throws) because the demonstrators are pretending to wear armor (*yoroi*), which makes their body movements (tai-sabaki) rigid. The kata is comprised of two sets and contains 21 techniques.

The first series is called *omote* (meaning "from the front") and has 14 movements. It is done at a rather slow pace with a pause after each of the sequences.

The second series is called *ura* (meaning "from behind") and comprises 7 movements. These seven movements are executed rapidly and without hesitation between sequences.

It should be noted that the techniques that comprise the 14 omote movements are grouped in pairs, each pair being the complement of the uneven number that precedes it.

KODOKAN GOSHIN-JUTSU

Translated as the "Kodokan's method of self-defense," this kata was invented in the '50s by a staff of masters at the Kodokan. Their intention was to update the techniques of the Kime-no-kata for modern times. This kata contains methods of throwing, holding, evading, kicking, striking, and choking. There are defenses against bare hands, sticks, knives, and guns.

JOSHI JUDO-GOSHIN-HO

Another kata invented during the '50s, the Kodokan's form of self-defense for women is a kata with the same intent as the Kodokan Goshin-jutsu, except that all techniques are designed strictly with a woman's physique in mind.

Since it would take a massive text to illustrate the 15 kata mentioned here, I have selected to illustrate in the rest of Part III those that are in my opinion the most important and the most representative. As Dr. Kano said, "The essence and beauty of judo lie in the kata; in them will you find the best means of finding the *way*. Study the kata and you will arrive at the truth and beauty of judo."

7
NAGE-NO-KATA
(FORMS OF THROWING)

GENERAL OUTLINE OF KATA

TE-WAZA (HAND TECHNIQUES)

1. *Uki-otoshi* (floating drop)
2. *Seoinage* (shoulder throw)
3. *Kata-guruma* (shoulder wheel)

KOSHI-WAZA (HIP THROWS)

4. *Uki-goshi* (floating hip throw)
5. *Harai-goshi* (sweeping hip throw)
6. *Tsuri-komi-goshi* (lift/pull hip throw)

ASHI-WAZA (LEG TECHNIQUES)

7. *Okuri-ashi-barai* (sweeping ankle throw)
8. *Sasae-tsuri-komi-ashi* (lift/pull ankle throw
9. *Uchi-mata* (inner thigh throw)

MA-SUTEMI-WAZA (REAR SACRIFICING THROW)

10. *Tomoe-nage* (circle throw)
11. *Ura-nage* (rear throw)
12. *Sumi-gaeshi* (corner throw)

YOKO-SUTEMI-WAZA (SIDE SACRIFICING THROW)

13. *Yoko-gake* (side hook)
14. *Yoko-guruma* (side wheel)
15. *Uki-waza* (floating technique)

Salutation

There are several ways of performing the opening honors of this kata, depending on the source and the organization under which one studied. Generally the opening salutation is as follows:

1. Tori and uke stand about 12–15 feet apart.
2. Both participants turn about 30 degrees and bow to the *joshi* (judge, masters observing, etc.). (Camera is in position of joshi. Thus all photos show the view from the judge's position.)
3. Now they face one another again. They bow to each other *(photo 7-1)*.
4. The participants assume a kneeling position and bow in *zarei*.[26]
5. Participants assume standing position.

Technique 1: Uki-Otoshi (Floating Drop)

Tori (man on right in photos) approaches uke as uke steps forward and seizes the gi in the classical *kumi-kata* *(photo 7-2)* position. As soon as the kumi-kata is secured, uke advances his right foot while tori withdraws his left foot a first time, then a second time, accentuating uke's right-foot disequilibrium. At the third step, tori pivots a quarter-turn to the left on his right foot and places his left knee on the ground *(photo 7-3)*, drawing the uke off balance and throwing him *(photo 7-4)*. Uke should land in classic *yoko-ukemi*[27] (side breakfall), tori remains upright *(photo 7-5)*.

Participants both stand up, facing opposite sides from the start of the technique, and execute exactly the same procedure on the opposite side. Participants both rise and return to start position (position in which salutation began).

Technique 2: Seoinage (Shoulder Throw)

Uke (man on left in photos) takes a big step forward with his left foot at the moment tori is moving toward him. Uke has brought his right arm behind him, readied in a fist. His intention is to strike tori on the head with the lower part of the fist *(photo 7-6)*.

Tori advances his right foot in front of the right foot of uke, who has taken a second step and rests on his right leg just before striking out at tori. As uke advances to strike, tori blocks the strike with his left forearm and leaps in toward advancing opponent *(photo 7-7)*. Tori's right arm is placed under opponent's right armpit, and tori throws uke with a right seoinage[16] throw *(photo 7-8)*, taking opponent to ground *(photo 7-9)*.

Participants stand and repeat the procedure on left side. Participants then assume a standing posture about six feet from one another.

7-1

7-2

7-3

7-4

7-5

7-6

7-7

7-8

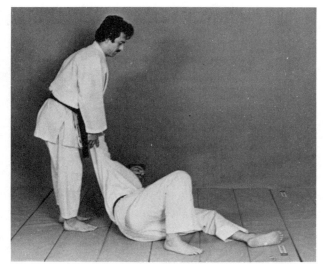

7-9

Technique 3: Kata-Guruma (Shoulder Wheel)

Participants assume a kumi-kata grasping position, as illustrated in photos. At the moment of the hold, tori's (man on right in photos) left hand winds around over uke's arm and grasps his gi near his biceps *(photo 7-10)*. This change of grip is sometimes accomplished after the participants take a first or second step toward tori's start position. On the third step tori lowers himself, taking advantage of opponent's forward motion *(photo 7-11)*, and lifts uke up on his shoulders and throws him with kata-guruma[28] *(photo 7-12)* to the mat *(photo 7-13)*.

Throw is repeated on left side with same preliminary actions. Participants return to start position. This completes the first section (te-waza).

Technique 4: Uki-Goshi (Floating Hip Throw)

Participants readjust their gi (uniforms) and sit a moment in zazen meditation (see Chapter 2). Tori (man on right in photos) advances toward uke until he is about 6 feet from him. Uke approaches tori in the same manner as Technique 2. As the uke attempts his striking action *(photo 7-14)*, tori pivots by placing his left foot forward and then moving to the rear with his right foot to place his left hip as an obstruction to the uke's movement. The uke's attempted striking action is thus parried *(photo 7-15)* and positioning is assumed for uki-goshi[29] technique *(photo 7-16)* which throws the opponent over the left hip and to the mat *(photo 7-17 and 7-18)*. Participants stand and repeat same actions on right side.

7-10

7-11

7-12

7-13

7-14

7-15

7-16

7-17

7-18

Technique 5: Harai-Goshi (Sweeping Hip Throw)

Participants stand and face each other and assume a standard kumi-kata position. Uke (man on left in photos) advances on tori as tori moves to rear. With this stepping action, tori slips his right hand under uke's left armpit and supports his palm against uke's left shoulderblade *(photo 7-19)*. On the third stepping action, tori pivots backward on his left foot and raises his right leg *(photo 7-20)*. Tori executes a harai-goshi[30] hip technique, sweeping the opponent's feet out from under him *(photo 7-21)* and throwing the uke to the mat *(photo 7-22)*.

Symmetrical execution then ensues to the left with necessary adjustments for performance on the opposite side.

Technique 6: Tsuri-Komi-Goshi (Lift/Pull Hip Throw)

Participants stand and face each other and assume a standard kumi-kata *(photo 7-23)* posture. With the first stepping action (uke [man on left in photos] advances toward tori as tori backsteps) tori places his left hand on uke's right lapel and grasps uke's left sleeve with right hand. On the third step, tori back-

pivots, raising his left arm high and obstructing uke with his left hip *(photo 7-24)*, throwing him over the hip *(photo 7-25)* with a tsuri-komi-goshi[31] to the mat *(photo 7-26)*.

Throw is then repeated on right side following same preliminary actions. This ends set two (koshi-waza). Participants return to start position *(photo 7-27)*.

Technique 7: Okuri-Ashi-Barai (Sweeping Ankle Throw)

After the participants adjust their gi (uniforms), tori (man on right in photos) walks up to uke, who awaits in a meditative state—calm/relaxed.

The performers grasp each other in kumi-kata posture and move slightly diagonally so uke's back is to *joshi* (which is at camera position) *(photo 7-28)*. Both take the traditional three steps toward tori's start position. With each step, however, the tori lifts the uke slightly higher, until the third step, when tori sweeps laterally from the left *(photo 7-29)* and sweeps opponent's feet out from under him *(photo 7-30)*, taking him to the mat *(photo 7-31)* in an okuri-ashi-barai[32] ankle sweep.

Throwing action is repeated on other side following all preliminary steps.

7-19

7-20

7-21

7-22

7-23

7-24

7-25

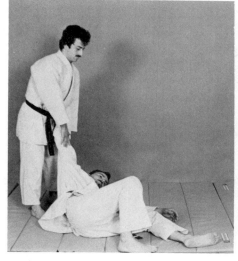

7-26

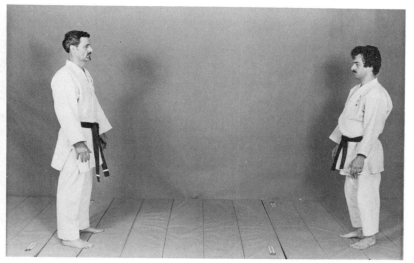

7-27

7-28

7-29

7-30

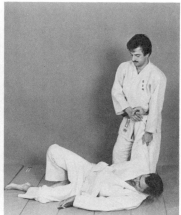

7-31

Technique 8: Sasae-Tsuri-Komi-Ashi (Lift/Pull Ankle Throw)

Assume standing posture at start position. Tori (man on right in photos) approaches uke and assumes a kumi-kata posture *(photo 7-32)*. Three traditional steps are taken by uke toward tori's start position. On the third step, tori interrupts uke's advance by placing his left foot as an obstruction at opponent's ankle *(photo 7-33)*, pulling him vigorously in a counterclockwise circle while sweeping his supporting foot off the mat *(photos 7-34 and 7-35)* in a sasae-tsuri-komi-ashi.[35]

Both participants stand and repeat the moves on opposite sides.

Technique 9: Uchi-Mata (Inner Thigh Throw)

Both participants return to start position. Tori (man on right in photos) approaches uke *(photo 7-36)* and assumes a kumi-kata position *(photo 7-37)*. However, the tori grasps the opponent's left lapel slightly higher (under chin or slightly around neck) with his right hand. Participants take three steps toward tori's start position. On the third step tori backsteps with left foot and slides right leg between uke's legs (some judoka prefer a leaping action, as illustrated here in *photo 7-38*,

which ends up in the classical setup in *photo 7-39)*. Because the uke has committed himself to a forward stepping action, he will be off balance forward, affording the tori the ability to sweep out his legs *(photo 7-40)* and throw him to the mat *(photo 7-41)* in uchi-mata.[34]

Repeat same movements on opposite side. This ends the third set, ashi-waza (leg throws). Return to start position.

Technique 10: Tomoe-Nage (Circle Throw)

Participants adjust their gi (uniforms) and sit in *zazen* meditation briefly. Upon standing, tori (man on right in photos) approaches uke and assumes kumi-kata position. Upon touching each other, uke pushes tori backward several times *(photo 7-42)*. Tori reacts and pushes uke several times again, returning him to his start position. Uke then strongly resists tori's pushing action, trying once more to make him retreat *(photo 7-43)*. Going with uke's pushing action, tori begins to drop to the mat, placing his foot on uke's abdomen *(photo 7-44)* and throwing him *(photo 7-45)* in a large circle to the mat behind tori *(photo 7-46)* (tomoe-nage[35]).

Repeat throw on opposite side following all preliminary movements.

7-32   7-33   7-34   7-35

7-36

7-37

7-38

7-39

7-40

7-41

7-42

7-43

7-44

7-45

7-46

Technique 11: Ura-Nage

Participants return to start position after tomoe-nage technique. Tori (man to right in photos) approaches uke and stops about six feet from him. Uke attacks him in the same manner as described for Technique 2 *(photo 7-47)*. Tori bends forward with his head lowered to dodge the blow. He places his right foot in front of uke's right foot, then places his left foot behind uke's right heel. Tori's head rests in front of uke and is pressed against his right pectoral. Tori's right arm holds uke's abdomen, the hand placed a little below the thorax, while his left arm circles opponent's waist and can—if desired—grasp the belt *(photo 7-48)*.

Tori times the uke's commitment of forward energy and throws his body backward, throwing the opponent off his feet *(photo 7-49)* and to the mat *(photo 7-50)* in ura-nage[36].

Repeat same procedure on opposite side following all preliminary actions. Return to start position.

Technique 12: Sumi-Gaeshi (Corner Throw)

Participants approach each other, meeting in mid-position *(photo 7-51)*, forming a *jigotai kumi-kata*[37] posture, turning so uke is at position of tori's start position and vice versa *(photo 7-52)*. (Tori is on right in photo 7-51, on left in rest of sequence) (*Note:* Some organizations teach that tori simply approaches uke at his start position and the two assume jigotai kumi-kata without turning to face opposite directions.)

Tori takes a small step backward with his right foot, and uke follows the movement with his left foot. Tori falls back another step with his left foot, and uke follows with his right foot. Their steps are semicircular from one side to another. Tori then advances his right foot to rest near uke's left foot (some schools teach placing the right foot deeply between the legs of opponent and not blocking his foot). Tori falls back *(photo 7-53)*, and his left instep lifts uke's right knee and thigh *(photo 7-54)*, throwing uke on his back *(photo 7-55)* (sumi-gaeshi)[38]. (*Note:* In some schools, the uke does not stay on the mat but rolls up into a standing posture.)

Repeat throw on opposite side with all preliminaries. This ends the fourth set, called ma-sutemi-waza (rear sacrificing throws). Participants return to start position and kneel.

7-47

7-48

7-49

7-50

7-51

7-52

7-53

7-54

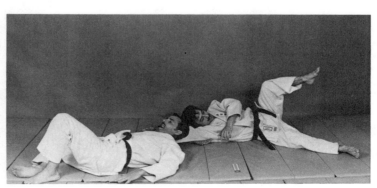

7-55

Technique 13: Yoko-Gake (Side Hooking Throw)

Participants adjust their gi (uniforms) and pause for a few moments of zazen (kneeling) meditation. Participants then stand.

Tori (man on right in photos) approaches uke and establishes kumi-kata posture *(photo 7-56)*. Tori falls back three successive steps. On the third step, right before uke is going to end it (*uke's back should be turned completely to the joshi [master] position; joshi posture represents camera position*), tori places his left foot on opponent's right ankle *(photo 7-57)*, falls back, and throws both of uke's feet out from under him *(photo 7-58)*, taking him to mat *(photo 7-59)* in classical yoko-gake[39] technique. (*Note:* Some schools teach this with tori knocking out only the right foot, not both.)

Repeat this throw on opposite side with all preliminary actions. Return to start position.

Technique 14: Yoko-Guruma (Side Wheel Throw)

Tori (man on right in photos) approaches uke, who attacks him in the sme manner as in Technique 2 *(photo 7-60)*. Tori evades with the exact technique from ura-nage (Technique 11). In fact, tori actually attempts a ura-nage *(photo 7-61)*. However, this time the uke anticipates the ura-nage and avoids the throwing action by leaning forward. Tori responds by falling back and pulling the uke in a counterclockwise circle *(photo 7-62)* throwing him to the side and onto the mat *(photo 7-63)* with yoko-guruma[40].

Uke rolls to standing position, and the same throwing action (with preliminaries) is repeated on opposite side. Participants return to start position.

Technique 15: Uki-Waza (Floating Throw)

Tori (man on right in photos) and uke follow same opening procedures as for sumi-gaeshi (Technique 12). On the third stepping action, tori slips his left leg (opened wide and stretched) *(photos 7-64 and 7-65)* to the outside of uke's right leg. Tori then falls on his left side *(photo 7-66)* and throws uke over his left shoulder to the mat *(photo 7-67)*. (Uki-waza[41]).

Execute the same technique on the opposite side, being sure to duplicate all preliminary procedures.

7-56

7-57

7-58

7-59

7-60

7-61

7-62

7-63

7-64

7-65

7-66

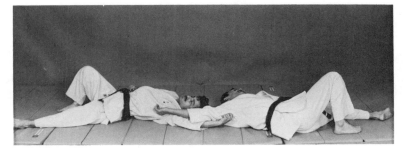

7-67

Ending Salutation

Both participants return to start position *(photo 7-68)*. They adjust their gi and bow to each other. They then bow to the joshi. Both participants assume a kneeling position and perform zazen meditation briefly. They end the kata with a *zarei* (kneeling bow).

A SPECIAL NOTE FROM MASTER ISAO OBATO

Nage-no-kata is done with slight degrees of variation around the world. In Japan, the kata is demonstrated pretty much as it is presented here; this version is also endorsed by the American Society of Classical Judoka.

However, some universities offer vast differences, even in Japan, the homeland of judo. In Europe and Canada, the kata is also slightly different.

One of the biggest differences is in the displacement of weight as well as in many variations of actual execution. Not all throws are repeated on both sides (left and right). Some are done only on one or the other.

This kata is unique because it not only teaches us to throw; it also instructs us in proper methods of body shifting (tai-sabaki), displacement of weight, and entry (tsukuri) into throwing actions.

The Nage-no-kata has a definite spirit: one of boldness and energy. It is with this spirit that this kata should be demonstrated.

7-68

8
GONOSEN-NO-KATA
(FORMS OF THROWS AND COUNTERTHROWS)

GENERAL OUTLINE OF KATA

IF THE UKE ATTACKS IN:	THEN THE TORI COUNTERS IN:
O-soto-gari (major outer sweep)	*O-soto-gari* (major outer sweep)
Hiza-guruma (knee wheel)	*Hiza-guruma* (knee wheel)
O-uchi-gari (major inside sweep)	*De-ashi-barai* (drawing ankle sweep)
De-ashi-barai (drawing ankle sweep)	*De-ashi-barai* (drawing ankle sweep)
Ko-soto-gake (minor outside hook)	*Tai-otoshi* (body drop)
Ko-uchi-gari (major inner sweep)	*Sasae-tsuri-komi-ashi* (lift/pull ankle sweep)
Koshi-guruma (hip wheel)	*Ushiro-goshi* (rear hip throw)
Koshi-guruma (hip wheel)	*Uki-goshi* (floating hip throw)
Hane-goshi (springing hip throw)	*Sasae-tsuri-komi-ashi* (lift/pull ankle sweep)
Harai-goshi (sweeping hip throw)	*Utsuri-goshi* (changing hip throw)
Uchi-mata (inner thigh throw)	*Sukui-nage* (scooping throw)
Ippon Seoinage (one-arm over-shoulder throw)	*Sumi-gaeshi* (corner throw)

Opening Salutation

Tori and uke stand about six feet apart, facing each other *(photo 8-1)*, and turn 30 degrees and bow to the *joshi* (judge, master observer). (*Note:* Camera is positioned at point where the joshi would sit.)

Participants face one another again and bow *(photo 8-2)*.

Note: Some schools use exactly the same opening as for Nage-no-kata.

Technique 1: O-Soto-Gari[42] as Counter to O-Soto-Gari

Participants approach each other, meet in middle of demonstration area, and assume kumi-kata posture *(photo 8-3)* the grasping position illustrated in photo. Uke (man on right in photos) moves in and attempts a left-sided o-soto-gari *(photo 8-4)*, which tori blocks with his abdomen, bending his legs to form a defensive (jigotai) posture[43]. Tori then executes his own o-soto-gari *(photo 8-5)*. Uke is too far advanced to resist the tori's attack and is thrown to the mat *(photos 8-6 and 8-7)*.

Technique 2: Hiza-Guruma[44] as Counter to Hiza-Guruma

Participants stand and resume kumi-kata position, but this time in different directions (tori is near uke's start position).

Uke (man on left in photos) attacks tori with a left hiza-guruma *(photo 8-8)*; that is, uke's left leg is on tori's right knee. Tori withdraws his leg a half-step to stop uke's initial attacking effort and unbalances uke to his right front. Tori then places his left foot on opponent's right leg *(photo 8-9)* and executes hiza-guruma *(photo 8-10)*, throwing uke to mat *(photo 8-11)*.

8-1

8-2

8-3

8-4

8-5

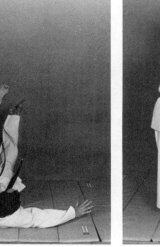

8-6

8-7

8-8

8-9

8-10

8-11

Technique 3: De-Ashi-Barai[45] as Counter to O-Uchi-Gari [46]

Uke (man on left in photos) rises from mat in the exact position he was thrown, with his back to joshi, and assumes kumi-kata posture with tori *(photo 8-12)*. Uke attacks with o-uchi-gari with his right leg on tori's left *(photo 8-13)*. Tori resists action with his abdomen; he flexes his right leg and carries the weight of his body as well as balancing on his right leg.

Tori pivots slightly to the left to accentuate the right front imbalance of uke, lifts him with combined effort of his forearms and wrists, and with his left leg sweeps uke's supporting foot *(photos 8-14 and 8-15)* right out from under him *(photo 8-16)*, throwing uke to the mat in a variation of de-ashi-barai *(photo 8-17)*.

Technique 4: De-Ashi-Barai[45] as Counter to De-Ashi-Barai

Uke (man on right in photos) immediately rises off mat and vigorously grasps tori's gi in kumi-kata *(photo 8-18)*. Tori advances his left foot, and uke attacks it with a de-ashi-barai with uke's right foot *(photo 8-19)*. Before tori's foot is swept too far, he lifts it up, allowing him to switch position on uke, making it tori's foot that is doing the sweeping and not uke's *(photo 8-20)*. Since uke has committed his leg to a sweeping action, the switch takes uke off guard, throwing him *(photo 8-21)* with de-ashi-barai to the mat *(photo 8-22)*.

8-12

8-13

8-14

8-15

8-16

8-17

8-18

(8-19

8-20

8-21

8-22

Technique 5: Tai-Otoshi[47]
as Counter to Ko-Soto-Gake[48]

Uke (man on right in photos) assumes standing position in the exact spot he landed in from the last throw. Tori should have his back toward joshi as they assume kumi-kata position (*photo 8-23*).

Uke attempts a ko-soto-gake with his left foot against tori's right foot (*photo 8-24*). Tori pivots a half-turn to his left and takes support on his left leg. With his hands, tori amplifies and deflects uke's frontal movement and moves in for tai-otoshi (*photo 8-25*), throwing

opponent into the air (*photo 8-26*) and to the mat (*photo 8-27*).

Technique 6: Sasae-Tsuri-Komi-Ashi[33]
as Counter to Ko-Uchi-Gari[17]

Uke (man on right in photos) stands, and participants join in kumi-kata posture (*photo 8-28*). Uke attacks, attempting to sweep tori's right foot with a right ko-uchi-gari (*photo 8-29*). Tori immediately places all his weight on his left foot and takes advantage of his opponent's one leg stance to place his right foot on uke's ankle (*photo 8-30*) and throws him (*photo 8-31*) with sasae-tsuri-komi-ashi (*photo 8-32*).

8-23

8-24

8-25

8-26

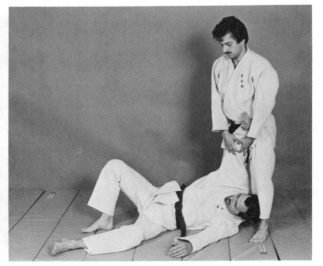

8-27

8-28

8-29

8-30

8-31

8-32

Technique 7: Ushiro-Goshi[49] as Counter to Koshi-Guruma[50]

Participants stand and grasp each other in kumi-kata position *(photo 8-33)*. Uke (man on right in photos) attacks tori with koshi-guruma *(photo 8-34)*. Tori, however, does not allow himself to be thrown off-balance forward; he resists with his abdomen, bends his legs, seizes uke's belt, and springs up on his legs while arching slightly backward, throwing opponent off his feet *(photo 8-35)* and to the mat *(photo 8-36)* with an ushiro-goshi.

Technique 8: Uki-Goshi[29] as Counter to Koshi-Guruma[50]

Uke (man on right in photos) stands, and both participants assume kumi-kata position *(photo 8-37)*. Uke attacks with a koshi-guruma *(photo 8-38)*. Tori blocks by resisting with his abdomen and lowering his body by bending the knees and pushes away uke's hips with his left hand. Tori then steps with his right foot in front of uke's right foot and makes a 180-degree counterclockwise pivot on the ball of the right foot *(photo 8-39)*, moving into position for an uki-goshi *(photo 8-40)*. Once in position, tori executes the throw *(photo 8-41)*, taking uke to the mat *(photo 8-42)*.

8-33

8-34

8-35

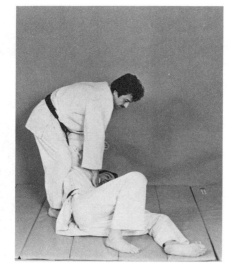

8-36

8-37

8-38

8-39

8-40

8-41

8-42

Technique 9: Sasae-Tsuri-Komi-Ashi[33] as Counter to Hane-Goshi[51]

Uke (man on right in photos) stands, and both participants assume kumi-kata posture *(photo 8-43)*. Uke attacks tori with hane-goshi *(photo 8-44)*. Tori blocks and dodges with body shifting to the right (tai-sabaki), very quickly advances his right foot, then his left, and displaces his hips with a small turning movement toward his right front. Tori then supports his weight on his left foot and positions himself for sasae-tsuri-komi-ashi *(photo 8-45)*. Tori sweeps opponent's feet out from under him *(photo 8-46)*, throwing him to the mat *(photo 8-47)*.

Technique 10: Utsuri-Goshi[52] as Counter to Harai-Goshi[30]

Uke (man on right in photos) assumes a standing posture and grasps tori in kumi-kata posture *(photo 8-48)*. Uke moves in for a harai-goshi *(photo 8-49)*, which the tori blocks with his abdomen, and lowers his body closer to the ground by bending his knees. Tori flexes his knees and arches his back, throwing the uke upward *(photos 8-50 and 8-51)*. As soon as uke is lifted, tori advances his left foot so as to place his hips under the stomach of uke, who is now beginning his descending movement. As uke lands, he lands on tori's left hip *(photo 8-52)* and is thrown over it *(photo 8-53)* to the mat *(photo 8-54)*.

8-43

8-44

8-45

8-46

8-47

8-48

8-49

8-50

8-51

8-52

8-53

8-54

Technique 11: Sukui-Nage[53]
as Counter to Uchi-Mata[54]

Uke (man on right in photos) assumes standing position and grasps tori in kumi-kata position *(photo 8-55)*. Uke attacks with an uchi-mata *(photo 8-56)*, which tori evades by flexing his abdomen, lowering his body by bending the knees, and placing the majority of his weight on his left leg. Uke places his foot down to keep his balance. When he does so, tori reaches between uke's legs with right hand, grasping a part of the gi *(photo 8-57)*, and scoops opponent up *(photo 8-58)* with a sukui-nage throw, taking uke to mat *(photo 8-59)*

Technique 12: Sumi-Gaeshi[38]
as Counter to Ippon Seoinage[55]

Uke (man on left in photos) assumes standing position and performers grip each other in kumi-kata position *(photo 8-60)*. Uke attacks with a right ippon seoinage *(photo 8-61)*. Tori very quickly makes a large rotational evading movement with a half-turn forward from right to left around uke's right hip *(photo 8-62)*. Tori places his left foot as an obstruction to uke's right foot and places his right instep on uke's inside upper left thigh. Tori continues to hold only uke's right arm (in some schools tori regrips uke in a more standard fashion) as he executes a sumi-gaeshi *(photo 8-63)*, taking uke to mat *(photo 8-64)*.

8-55

8-56

8-57

8-58

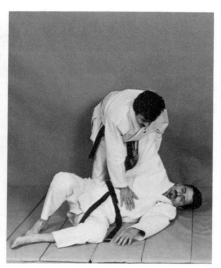

8-59

8-60

8-61

8-62

8-63

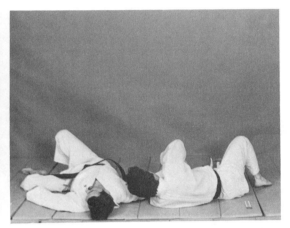

8-64

Ending Salutation

Tori and uke slowly rise to their feet, facing each other *(photo 8-65)*. Participants then return to their original start position, readjust their gi, execute a rei (bow) to each other and then to the joshi.

Important note: In order to demonstrate the spectacular beauty of this kata, perfect understanding between tori and uke is necessary. Each must know what the other is going to do. The tempo of this kata is fast, so timing and realistic execution are essential.

There is only a slight pause between the end of the last technique and the gripping action of the technique to come. All other moves are done smoothly and quickly. For the sake of realism, the uke must attack with

8-65

vigor and sincerity. He must anticipate the throw and execute a perfect breakfall (ukemi) to give the throwing action more beauty.

9
KIME-NO-KATA
(FORMS OF SELF-DEFENSE)

GENERAL OUTLINE OF KATA

IDORI (SEATED DEFENSES)

1. *Ryote-dori* (both-hand seizure)
2. *Tsukikata* (straight punch to stomach)
3. *Suri-age* (blow against forehead with palm)
4. *Yoko-uchi* (blow at the temple)
5. *Ushiro-dori* (shoulder grab from behind)
6. *Tsuki-komi* (direct downward cut with dagger)
7. *Yoko-tsuki* (side thrust with dagger)

TACHIAI (STANDING DEFENSES)

1. *Ryote-dori* (both-hand seizure)
2. *Sode-tori* (sleeve seizure)
3. *Tsuki-kake* (straight punch to face)
4. *Suri-age* (blow against forehead with palm)
5. *Tsuki-age* (uppercut)
6. *Yoko-uchi* (side blow to temple)
7. *Keage* (front kick defense)
8. *Ushiro-dori* (shoulder grab from behind)

9. *Tsuki-komi* (thrust to stomach with dagger)
10. *Kiri-komi* (direct downward cut with dagger)
11. *Nuki-kake* (sword unsheathing)
12. *Kiri-otoshi* (direct downward cut with sword)

Opening Salutation

Participants stand about 12 feet apart facing each other *(photo 9-1)*. Tori is to the right of joshi (judge, master observer, etc.; camera is positioned at joshi), and uke is to the left. They bow *(photo 9-2)*.

Participants then turn 30 degrees to joshi and bow. It should be noted that uke is holding in his hands a *katana* (sword) and a *tanto* (knife). They are held at waist level with handles toward tori and blades facing upward.

Participants kneel *(photo 9-3)*. As uke kneels, he places his weapons at his right side, both with handles facing tori and blade edges facing uke. They bow *(photo 9-4)*.

Uke then takes up weapons in his right hand, stands *(photo 9-5)*, turns, and kneels again, placing weapons behind him with handles toward joshi and blade edges toward himself *(photos 9-6 and 9-7)*.

Both participants stand and approach one another *(photo 9-8)*, meeting in middle of demonstration area. They kneel again about eight inches from one another and bow once more, using only thumb and index finger on mat (called *hiza-zume*). Participants should bow their heads to the left (some schools say to the right) to avoid hitting each other in the head *(photo 9-9)*. Both resume sitting posture with palms on thighs.

9-1

9-2

9-3

9-4

9-5

9-6

9-7

9-8

9-9

IDORI

Technique 1: Ryote-Dori

Participants are kneeling, facing one another (called *taiza*). Uke (man on left in photos) reaches forward and briskly grasps tori's wrists *(photo 9-10)*. Tori takes support on the left leg and delivers a front kick (*mae-geri*) to uke's midsection, simultaneously drawing uke's hands apart *(photo 9-11)*. Tori places his right leg down and then places his right knee down and lifts his left knee. While he is doing the knee movement, tori secures a *hara-gatame* (stomach armlock) *(photo 9-12)*.

Technique 2: Tsukikata

Participants resume *taiza* posture, but this time they are about 1½ feet from each other. Uke (man on left in photos) draws back his right fist *(photo 9-13)*and thrusts it straight out at tori. Tori dodges it by stepping to the side and up on his left leg while deflecting the punch with his left hand and delivering his own punch to uke's face with his right hand *(photo 9-14)*. Tori turns to uke's side by lifting right knee and going down on left knee. Simultaneously, he secures a *kuzure-hara-ga-tame* (variation on stomach lock) in which tori's left arm applies a neck lock on uke's neck and places uke's elbow across his stomach. Pressure is applied by drawing up on elbow while pushing down with stomach *(photo 9-15)*.

Technique 3: Suri-Age

Participants resume taiza position *(photo 9-16)*. Uke (man on left in photos) pushes off with a palm heel (*teisho*) strike to opponent's chin/nose in an effort to throw back the head and dislocate the neck. Tori rises and moves to the side and back in order to evade the force of the attack. At the same time, tori grasps uke's striking arm and delivers a front kick to uke's solar plexus *(photo 9-17)*. (Note: There is an upward pull on uke's striking hand as tori delivers the kick. This upward movement not only dissipates the force of the blow but also sends the uke off balance forward.)

Tori pivots to uke's right side, bringing his arm down *(photo 9-18)* and slamming opponent's face into the mat. Tori maintains a hold on uke's arm in order to exert pinning pressure. Uke surrenders, tapping the mat twice *(photo 9-19)*.

9-10

9-11

9-12

9-13

9-14

9-15

9-16

9-17

9-18

9-19

Technique 4: Yoko-Uchi

Participants resume taiza posture. Uke (man on left in photos) makes a fist with right hand *(photo 9-20)* and swings it with the intent of striking the tori on the left temple with the bottom edge of his hand. Tori dodges the attack by bending from the waist to left rear while rising on left leg. Simultaneously, he slips his head under uke's right arm so as to block opponent's motion; tori's right arm passes in front of uke's head and left cheek to pin uke's head to right shoulder. Finally tori's left palm, palm flat, is pressed behind uke's right hip (or else it can grasp tori's right wrist, as illustrated in *photo 9-21*). Tori throws uke back to the mat and assumes a hold-down type position that is very similar to a kata-gatame[56] *(photo 9-22)*. Tori immediately raises his chest, locks uke's arm around his neck with his left hand *(photo 9-23)*, and delivers a downward elbow strike (*omote-hiji-uchi*) with right elbow *(photo 9-24)*

Technique 5: Ushiro-Dori

Tori resumes a kneeling (seiza) posture in his start position. Uke circles around behind him and assumes seiza posture (putting him on the right in photos) *(photo 9-25)*.

Uke rises from the waist and secures a choke hold around tori's neck with his right arm. Tori grasps the uke's right arm with his right hand and places his left hand on mat for support (or, if desired, tori can grasp uke's right arm with *both* hands) *(photo 9-26)*. Tori shifts right hip forward, left hip to the rear, simultaneously swinging *slightly* upward and pulling the uke's right arm. This action will throw uke over tori's shoulder *(photo 9-27)* and to the mat *(photo 9-28)*. Tori continues body momentum that was created with force of the throw and rolls to his left side *(photo 9-29)*, delivering a downward punch (*omote-seiken-uchi*) to uke's solar plexus *(photo 9-30)*.

9-20

9-21

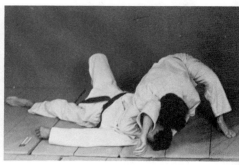

9-22

9-23

9-24

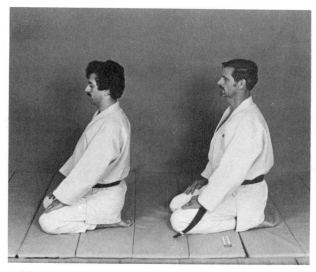

9-25

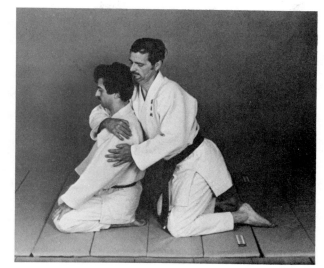

9-26

9-27

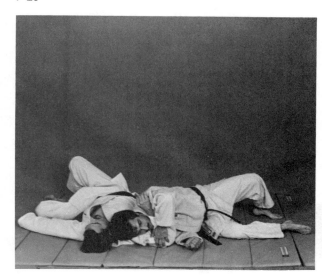

9-28

9-29

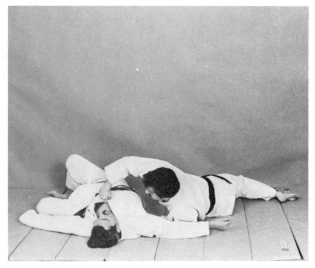

9-30

Technique 6: Tsuki-Komi

Participants resume taiza position. Uke (man on left in photos) stands, turns around (facing his start position), and walks to the weapons he placed down on the mat earlier. He kneels, takes up the dagger, and places it, with cutting edge upward, deeply inside the left flap of his gi above his belt so that it is not visible to the eye. Uke stands and returns to tori, kneeling down about 20 inches from him, and resumes taiza posture *(photo 9-31)*. Uke reaches into his belt and draws out the dagger with his right hand, bringing it to his right thigh *(photo 9-32)*. Uke thrusts forward with the dagger *(photo 9-33)*. As he does so, tori sidesteps the action, going up on his right knee to opponent's right side *(photo 9-34)*, and applies a *hara-gatame* (see Technique 2 for more detail on this holding technique) *(photo 9-35)*.

Technique 7: Kiri-Komi

Participants resume taiza posture *(photo 9-36)*. (*Note*: In some schools, the participants sit at opposite ends in this opening position.

That is, uke is at tori's start position and vice versa.)

Uke (man on left in photos) has replaced the dagger in his gi at the end of the last sequence. He now unsheaths the weapon and aggressively begins a downward cut *(photo 9-37)* with the intent of cutting tori on head. As uke's arm descends, tori sidesteps to uke's right, going up on his right knee and catching uke's arm with his outstretched arms *(photo 9-38)*, and locks opponent's arm when it reaches its full descent *(photo 9-39)*. Uke slaps twice to surrender. Uke returns weapon to his left side (inside gi).

Technique 8: Yoko-Tsuki

Both participants resume taiza posture. Then tori (in front in photos), staying in his position, turns 180 degrees to face his start position. Uke stands and kneels at tori's left side. They are thus showing their right profile to joshi (in some schools, they show their left profile, tori does not turn, and uke simply kneels at his right side) *(photo 9-40)*.

Uke unsheaths his dagger and attacks tori

9-31

9-32

9-33

9-34

9-35

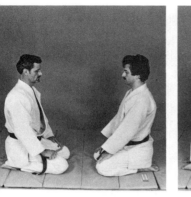

9-36

9-37

9-38

9-39

9-40

9-41

9-42

9-43

9-44

with a thrust to his left side *(photo 9-41)*. Tori parries the attack with his left hand and punches uke in the face with his right hand *(photo 9-42)*. Tori immediately applies a *hara-gatame* (see Technique 2 for more details on this hold) *(photo 9-43)*.

Uke taps mat twice to surrender. Tori resumes a seated posture with uke in the middle of demonstration area. (*Note:* Uke has replaced the dagger inside the left side of his gi.) Both participants stand and return to start position. Tori resumes a standard kneeling posture. Uke turns toward the sword, which is still on the mat, kneels, and puts the dagger back in place *(photo 9-44)*. Uke turns back toward tori in a kneeling position (seiza). This ends the kneeling (idori) portion of the *Kime-no-kata.*

TACHIAI

Both participants stand and approach each other in the middle of the mat *(photo 9-45)*. (When standing from a kneeling position always get up with the right leg first.)

Technique 1: Ryote-Dori

Uke (man on left in photos) seizes tori's wrists in a normal two-hand hold *(photo 9-46)*. Tori retreats one step with left foot and delivers a front kick *(mae-geri-kaeri)* to uke's midsection *(photo 9-47)*. Immediately, tori secures an underarm lock on uke's left arm *(photo 9-48)*. Uke taps tori twice on leg to surrender.

Technique 2: Sode-Tori

Tori and uke return to a position facing each other. Tori (man on right in photos) then turns around, looking in the direction of his start position. Uke approaches him and grasps his left sleeve *(photo 9-49)*. (*Note:* In some schools, the tori remains where he is and the uke circles around him and grasps his left sleeve.)

Both take two steps forward, and tori goes

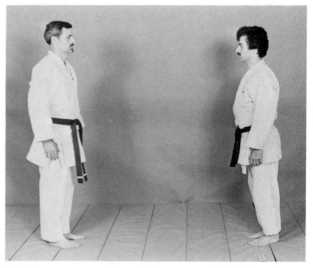

9-45

along with uke's stepping, timing the exact moment to pivot clockwise (on uke's second step) *(photo 9-50)* and execute an o-soto-gari[42] on uke's right leg *(photo 9-51)*, taking him into the air *(photo 9-52)* and to the mat *(photo 9-53)*.

Note: Some schools wait until the third stepping action by uke to pivot into o-soto-gari. In addition, some schools deliver a low-level right-heel kick to the side of uke's right knee.

9-46

9-47

9-48

9-49

9-50

9-51

9-52

9-53

Technique 3: Tsuki-Kake

Uke (man on right in photos) rises off the mat, and both participants switch start positions (uke is where tori normally starts and vice versa). (*Note:* Some schools *do not* switch positions on this movement.) Uke draws back his right arm in a fist and prepares to strike tori in the face with a straight punching attack *(photo 9-54)*.

Uke punches and, as he does so, steps forward with his right foot. During this punching action, tori steps to the left, out of the way of punch, and guides the punch to safety with his right hand *(photo 9-55)*. Since uke has committed himself to a straight punch, by missing the target he has left himself off balance. Tori aids in throwing him off balance forward by pulling down on his right arm and placing his left hand at uke's left lapel *(photo 9-56)*. The uke's instinctive reaction will be to pull up. When he does so tori goes with the action and applies a *hadaka-jime* choking position,[57] being sure to pull the uke violently backward. Uke surrenders by

stamping twice with his right foot *(photo 9-57)*.

Technique 4: Tsuki-Age

This attacking action is commonly defined as an "uppercut with the fist." However, more recently the action is being substituted by an "upward palm heel." This change, however, is not universally followed in judo.

Participants again start in opposite directions (see opening of Technique 3, "Tsuki-kake") about one yard apart *(photo 9-58)*. Uke (man on right in photos) steps back with his right foot *(photo 9-59)* and then steps forward, delivering an upward palm heel strike (or punch) at tori. Tori rapidly dodges by leaning backward and then grasps uke's right wrist with both hands pulling upward (with uke's momentum) to throw him off balance forward *(photo 9-60)*. Tori pivots to uke's right side and applies an underarm lock *(photo 9-61)*. Uke surrenders by tapping tori's left thigh with his left hand.

9-54

9-55

9-56

9-57

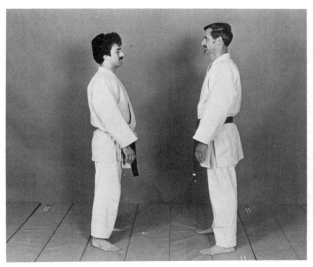

9-58

9-59

9-60

9-61

Technique 5: Suri-Age

Participants again begin by facing opposite directions *(photo 9-62)*. Uke (man on right in photos) attempts a palm heel strike to tori's upper lip or chin. Tori withdraws his right foot, leans slightly back (to evade force of attack), and simultaneously blocks the striking arm upward and delivers a straight punch (for more detail on punching tools and techniques, see Part IV) to uke's midsection *(photos 9-63 and 9-64)*. Immediately, tori pivots in *(photo 9-65)* and executes a left-sided o-goshi, which takes uke over his hip *(photo 9-66)* and to the mat *(photo 9-67)*.

Technique 6: Yoko-Uchi

Participants face each other in opposite start position corners about one yard apart *(photo 9-68)*. Uke (man on right in photos)

steps back on right foot, readying his fist for a hooking circular strike to tori's face *(photo 9-69)*. (*Note:* Some schools use a downward strike.)

As the circular strike is attempted, tori steps to his left side with his left foot and ducks under the uke's fist *(photo 9-70)*. With his right hand, tori grasps uke's left lapel as he steps around to his rear. At the same time, since the uke missed his target, the force of his initial swing brings uke's right arm in a circle *(photo 9-71)*. Tori catches uke's right arm with his left hand and secures a kuzure okuri-eri-jime *(photo 9-72)*.

Choking is applied by pulling back on uke's right arm and down and back on his left lapel (the lapel actually chokes the side of his neck). (*Note:* Some schools apply a standard okuri-eri-jime[59] instead of the technique illustrated.) Uke surrenders by striking the mat twice with his right foot.

9-62

9-63

9-64

9-65

9-66

9-67

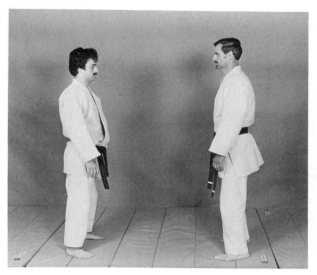

9-68

9-69

9-70

9-71

9-72

Technique 7: Ke-Age

Participants again stand in opposite start positions *(photo 9-73)*. Uke (man on right in photos) takes support on his left leg and attempts a front kick (mae-geri) to tori's groin. Tori backsteps to the left side with his right foot, dodging the attack as he parries the foot away with his left hand *(photo 9-74)*, seizing the ankle. Then tori pulls the kicking leg out to his left side *(photo 9-75)* and delivers a front kick of his own to uke's groin *(photo 9-76)*.

Technique 8: Ushiro-Dori

Participants assume start position, facing each other. Tori (man on right in photos) then turns to face his formal start position (back to uke). Both begin to advance, starting with the

right foot. On the third step, uke reaches around tori *(photo 9-77)*, but tori prevents a secure hold by raising his arms, grasping uke's right arm *(photo 9-78)*. Tori lowers himself on his right knee *(photo 9-79)* and throws uke over his shoulder *(photo 9-80)* to the mat *(photo 9-81)*. Before uke can get up, tori delivers a knife hand strike (see Part IV) to the base of uke's nose *(photo 9-82)*.

Technique 9: Tsuki-Komi

Participants return to start position about one yard from each other. Uke (man on left in photos) turns and returns to formal start position (where he initially started kata), faces away from tori, and kneels down at weapons. Uke picks up dagger *(photo 9-83)* and places it in his belt, cutting edge up, on his left side. Uke rises, turns to face tori, and stands in front of him about one yard away. Uke unsheaths his dagger *(photo 9-84)* and attempts a straight thrust to tori's abdomen. Tori steps to his left side by backstepping with his right leg, dodging the dagger thrust and parrying the hand with tori's left hand. Simultaneous with the parry, tori delivers a punch to uke's face *(photo 9-85)*. Tori immediately steps to uke's side and secures a hara-gatame (stomach arm lock) *(photo 9-86)*. Uke taps tori's left thigh twice to surrender. Uke returns dagger to left side of his belt.

9-74   9-75   9-76

9-77

9-78

9-79

9-80

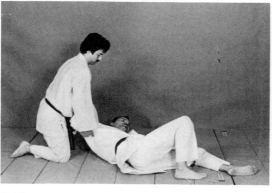

9-81

9-82

9-83

9-84

9-85

9-86

Technique 10: Kiri-Komi

Participants resume start position in opposite corners *(photo 9-87)*. Uke (man on right in photos) steps back on right foot and draws dagger out of his belt and over head in an attempt to cut/stab opponent on the head *(photo 9-88)*. As uke attempts to stab, tori moves to his left side, allowing the dagger to pass his head, at the same time parrying the arm with his left hand and punching uke in face from under uke's right armpit *(photo 9-89)*. Trapping uke's arm *(photo 9-90)*, tori secures an arm lock *(photo 9-91)*. Uke strikes mat twice with his left foot to surrender.

Technique 11: Nuki-Kake

Participants resume standard start position. Uke (man on left in photos) turns with back to tori, walks over to sword, and kneels, returning dagger to position. He then picks up the sword *(photo 9-92)* as follows:

Uke's left hand, palm up, grasps the top of the scabbard (saya) while his right hand, palm down, passes above the left hand to take hold of the handle of the sword right near where the handle and scabbard join. In these two complementary movements, the thumbs are placed in opposition in relation to the other fingers.

Uke arranges the sword perpendicular to the mat by letting the end of the scabbard press against the mat, his left hand (without altering its hold) sliding down to the bottom of the scabbard. Then he lifts the sword only in order to slip it into his belt from the left-hand side and keeps it there with cutting edge facing up. Uke continues to hold the sword in his left hand.

Tori turns and faces his initial start position. Uke steps around him so that they are about a yard and a half apart *(photo 9-93)*. Uke steps to the rear with his left foot and begins to draw his sword out of the scabbard. Tori advances forward with a big step of his left foot and blocks the drawing movement with his right hand *(photos 9-94 and 9-95)*. Tori steps behind uke, placing his right arm up and under uke's right arm *(photo 9-96)*, and secures a kata-ha-jime[23] choke *(photo 9-97)*. Uke surrenders by stamping the mat twice with his right foot.

9-87

9-88

9-89

9-90

9-91

9-92

9-93

9-94

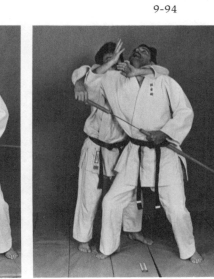

9-95

9-96

9-97

Technique 12: Kiri-Otoshi

Participants return to start position in opposite corners about nine feet apart. Uke (man on right in photos) unsheaths his sword *(photo 9-98)* and holds it in a *chu-dan* (mid-level) start position *(photo 9-99)*. Uke raises the sword above his head and advances two steps toward tori *(photo 9-100)*.

Uke executes a downward slash at tori. Tori steps to uke's side, allowing the sword to pass to his side and at the same time grasping uke around the neck with his left arm and on the right wrist with his right arm *(photo 9-101)*. Tori secures a hara-gatame hold *(photo 9-102)*.

9-98

9-99

9-100

9-101

9-102

9-103

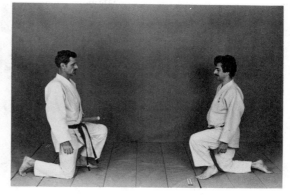

9-104

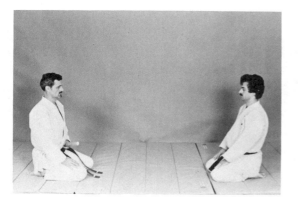

9-105

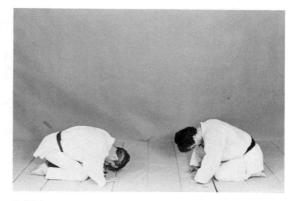

9-106

Ending Salutation

Participants return to standard position nine feet from one another as uke (man on left in photos) returns the sword to its scabbard *(photo 9-103)*. Both kneel *(photo 9-104)* in formal seiza posture *(photo 9-105)* and bow *(photo 9-106)*. Participants stand and return to formal start position (the position in which they began the kata, about 12–15 feet apart).

Tori remains standing. Uke kneels with back to tori, facing the weapons. He removes the sword and places it in his right hand and picks up dagger and does the same (see Opening Salutation for details on how to hold the weapons). Uke stands to face tori. Both bow to each other, standing, and then turn 30 degrees and bow to joshi. They face each other again. This ends the Kime-no-kata.

10
ITSUTSU-NO-KATA
(FORMS OF FIVE)

General Outline of Kata

There are no specific names for the various movements of this kata. Instead, the movements are based on various principles, and it is these principles that are outlined below.

1. Concentration of energy and action.
2. Reaction and nonresistance.
3. Cyclic principle of circular dissipation of energy. Also known as the *principle of the whirlwind.*
4. Alternation of the pendulum.
5. Principle of the void; of emptiness.

Opening Salutation

Participants stand 12 feet apart. Both pivot 30 degrees and bow to joshi (judges, master observer, etc.; camera is in position of joshi). They face each other again and bow *(photo 10-1).*

Technique 1: Principle of Concentration of Energy and of Direct Action

Uke (man on right in photos) does not move. Tori approaches him slowly, closes his fingers to keep his palm flat, and raises his right hand as he advances slowly forward. Tori comes right up to uke and places his hand in middle of uke's sternum *(photo 10-2).*

Tori advances his left foot and presses his hand against uke, who begins to step back slowly. Tori continues to push slowly against uke, who is now trying very hard to keep his balance, and slowly he starts to accelerate his walking until he takes a large step and extends his right arm. Since uke never regained his balance, he falls backward *(photo 10-3)* to the mat like a dead tree falling *(photo 10-4).*

Upon impact with mat, uke sits up with legs extended and hands on knees.

Technique 2: Principle of Reaction and of Nonresistance

Uke (man on right in photos) starts from the seated position in which he ended up after Technique 1. He rises slowly to a high kneeling posture to the left (that is, right knee still on the ground). His left palm is on left knee, and his right hand is held straight out at tori (almost like extending a dagger).

Uke stands up. He advances his right foot

10-1

10-2

10-3

10-4

with a big step forward toward tori and stretches his right arm as if to strike tori in the stomach with the tips of the fingers. Tori has not yet moved since Technique 1. Tori pivots to the left and withdraws his left foot to dodge uke's attack *(photo 10-5)*. Tori seizes uke's arm *(photo 10-6)*, pulling him forward as he back-pivots and kneels, throwing opponent with an uki-otoshi[60] technique *(photos 10-7 and 10-8)*.

After impact with mat, uke assumes a sitting position on mat with legs straight and hands on knees.

Technique 3: Principle of Circular Energy and Dissipation *or* of the Whirlwind

Both participants assume the same kneeling position as described at the beginning of Technique 2. They get up together, bend forward, and extend their arms like the wings of a bird *(photo 10-9)*. Participants then perform—arms extended—two symmetrical complementary circles with their bodies. The circles are about six feet in diameter and connected like the lower and upper loops of a figure eight. Both participants meet in center of mat (center of whirlwind) with wrists touching *(photo 10-10)*.

Suddenly tori lets himself fall *(photo 10-11)*

to his back and left side, his legs extended far forward and in contact with uke's legs. Tori uses his hands to throw uke over him *(photo 10-12)*. Uke falls forward and up to a standing position *(photo 10-13)*.

Technique 4: Principle of Alternation of the Pendulum

Uke (man on right in photos) has ended Technique 3 with his back toward tori. Tori stands and leans body forward *(photo 10-14)*, coming to a position in which his arms are parallel with his hips. Tori then raises his arms crosswise (across his chest) and extended like a bird about to take flight. Tori then advances toward uke with rapid steps until he comes to uke's left side. Tori actually passes uke by one step and then raises his arms obliquely above his shoulders and separated *(photo 10-15)*. Tori brings his center of gravity to a rooted posture by concentrating on his abdomen and pressing his heels into the mat. Suddenly, tori begins to backstep and carries uke along in his retreat. Uke is progressively unbalanced backward. Then, tori drops to his left knee and swings his arm back, throwing uke off his feet *(photo 10-16)*.

Uke assumes a sitting position on mat with legs outstretched and hands on knees. Tori stays in kneeling position, facing away from uke, and lowers his arms to his side.

10-5

10-6

10-7

10-8

10-9

10-10

10-11

10-12

10-13

10-14

10-15

10-16

Technique 5: Principle of Void *or* of Emptiness

Tori (man on right in photos) comes to a standing position, as does uke (with his back toward tori). Both advance their right foot and extend their arms like a bird in flight, leaning forward *(photo 10-17)* (*Note:* Some schools stay erect rather than bending forward.)

Both participants move in a figure eight pattern as for Technique 3 *(photo 10-18)*. When they meet and are about to collide, tori very rapidly lets himself fall to the mat on his side (in some schools, on his back) with his legs together. Uke cannot step over the barrier *(photo 10-19)* and is thrown over it *(photo 10-20)* to the mat *(photo 10-21)*. Uke immediate comes to his feet.

Ending Salutation

Tori (man on left in photos) then stands *(photo 10-22)*, and both return to start position. They readjust their gi (uniform) and bow to each other, standing *(photo 10-23)*. Both participants turn 30 degrees and bow to joshi. They then face each other again. This ends Itsutsu-no-kata.

10-17

10-18

10-19

10-20

10-21

10-22

10-23

11
KOSHIKI-NO-KATA
(FORMS OF ANTIQUITY)

GENERAL OUTLINE OF KATA

SERIES 1 (14 MOVEMENTS): OMOTE

1. *Tai*, starting position
2. *Yume-no-uchi*, the dream
3. *Ryokuhi*, to master his strength
4. *Mizu-guruma*, the waterwheel
5. *Mizu-nagare*, the stream
6. *Hiki-otoshi*, to pull and make fall
7. *Kodaore*, the tree trunk
8. *Uchi-kudaki*, to pulverize
9. *Tani-otoshi*, fall in valley
10. *Kuruma-daoshi*, thrown-down wheel
11. *Shikoro-dori*, hold onto shoulder piece (of armor, not skin)
12. *Shikoro-gaeshi*, overturning by shoulder piece (on armor)
13. *Yudachi*, evening rain
14. *Taki-otoshi*, the cascade

SERIES 2 (7 MOVEMENTS): URA

1. *Mi-kudaki*, to reduce the body to powder
2. *Kuruma-gaeshi*, to revolve like a wheel
3. *Mizu-iri*, to follow the current
4. *Ryu-setsu*, snow on the willow
5. *Saka-otoshi*, to throw down the slope
6. *Yuki-ore*, branch broken under weight of snow
7. *Iwa-nami*, wave against the rock

Opening Salutation

Participants stand approximately 15 feet apart *(photo 11-1)* and bow to each other *(photo 11-2)*. They turn 45 degrees *(photo 11-3)* and bow *(photo 11-4)* to joshi (judge, master observer; remember that the camera is positioned at the joshi).

11-1

11-2

11-3

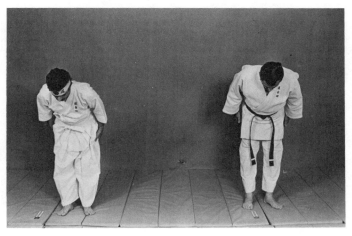

11-4

OMOTE

Technique 1: Tai

It is important to remember that the participants in the kata are both supposed to be clad in traditional armor (yoroi). After bowing to joshi, uke (man on right in photos) turns back to formal start position. Tori, instead of turning back, advances forward on his left foot *(photo 11-5)*. This is start position for first technique *(photo 11-6)*. Uke advances forward toward tori with slight diagonal movement *(photo 11-7)* to place himself a little in front of tori. When uke's right foot has come alongside of tori he grasps tori's belt both in front and in back *(photo 11-8)* and raises his left leg at a right angle *(photo 11-9)*.

Uke attempts to throw tori to ground by twisting his hips. Tori blocks uke's hip movement with his right hand and places his left hand on uke's collarbone *(photo 11-10)*. Tori backsteps a few short steps while twisting opponent to put him off balance *(photo 11-11)*. When uke is off balance, tori assumes a kneeling position, twists his body counterclockwise, and throws uke to rear *(photo 11-12)* onto his back *(photo 11-13)*. *Remember:* In theory, the idea of the throw is to throw uke back onto his head, causing a fracture of the spine (because of the excessive weight of the armor on uke.)

Uke assumes a seated posture on mat *(photo 11-14)* and then comes up to stand.

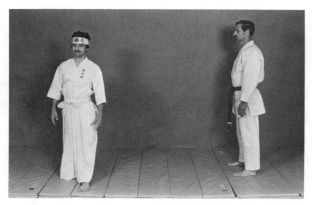

11-5

11-6

11-7

11-8

11-9

11-10

11-11

11-12

11-13

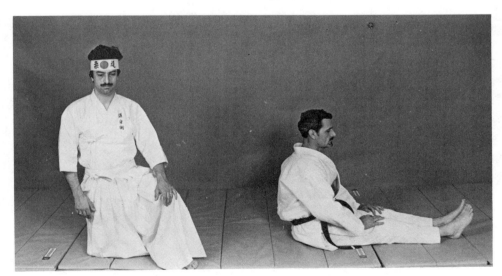

11-14

Technique 2: Yume-No-Uchi

From start position as in Technique 1 (Tai) *(photo 11-15)*, uke (man on left in photos) approaches tori in the exact same manner, grasping his belt with both hands and lifting left foot *(photo 11-16)*. Tori initially attempts the same movement as in Technique 1, but this time the uke resists with his abdomen and lowers his center of gravity by bending his knees and concentrating *(photo 11-17)*. Tori immediately takes advantage of this to pass around his right hip and recede (backstep) with small steps in order to unbalance uke forward and finally throw him with a modified yoko-guruma[40] *(photos 11-18 and 11-19)* on his side *(photo 11-20)*. Uke immediately comes to a standing posture while tori remains outstretched on mat for a moment *(photo 11-21)*.

Technique 3: Ryokuhi

Tori (man on left in photos) returns to start position with uke on opposite side *(photo 11-22)*. Uke takes a step forward with left foot and then with right and reaches out to grasp tori's belt *(photo 11-23)*. Tori dodges by withdrawing a step and passes around to uke's rear *(photo 11-24)*, out of uke's reach; to assure that uke can't grasp his belt, he blocks uke's hands with his right hand. Stepping to uke's back with slight bias to his left side, tori places his hands on uke's upper arm and shoulder *(photo 11-25)*. With his body up against uke's, tori drops to his left knee and throws opponent over his raised right knee *(photos 11-26 and 11-27)* crashing uke to the mat *(photo 11-28)*. Uke assumes a sitting posture and then stands.

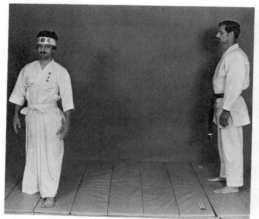

11-15

11-16

11-17

11-18

11-19

11-20

11-21

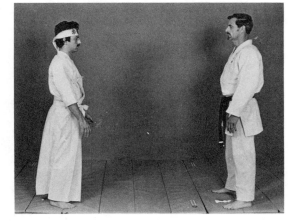

11-22

11-23

11-24

11-25

11-26

11-27

11-28

Technique 4: Mizu-Guruma

Participants assume same start position as in Technique 3 *(photo 11-29)*, and uke (man on right in photos) initiates same attack as in Technique 3 *(photo 11-30)* while tori attempts the same response as in Technique 3 *(photo 11-31)*. However, this time uke anticipates the backward throw and uke stands erect, resisting the movement. Taking advantage of this resistance, tori falls to mat *(photo 11-32)* and executes a yoko-guruma[40] *(photo 11-33)*, which throws uke to mat *(photo 11-34)*. Uke assumes a standing position as tori lies outstretched on the mat momentarily *(photo 11-35)*.

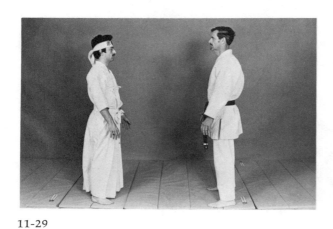

11-29

11-30

11-31

11-32

11-33

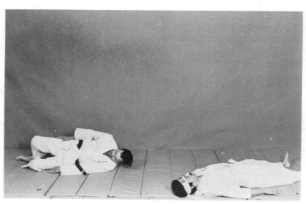

11-34

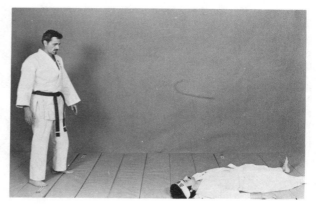

11-35

Technique 5: Mizu-Nagare

Tori (man on right in photos) assumes a standing posture and circles around to start position *(photos 11-36 and 11-37)*. Participants are about 10 feet apart. Both walk toward each other with majestic steps. Tori stops when uke is two paces from him. Uke in turn makes a gesture with his right hand as if he removed a dagger from his belt and is extend-ing his left hand to grab tori's collar to better thrust him in the abdomen. Tori slightly bends his upper body to dodge the attack. Uke reaches out to grab tori *(photo 11-38)*. Tori seizes his arm, backsteps *(photos 11-39)*, and pulls uke off balance, forcing him to fall *(photo 11-40)* to the ground *(photo 11-41)*. Uke sits up on the mat *(photo 11-42)*, and participants assume a starting position.

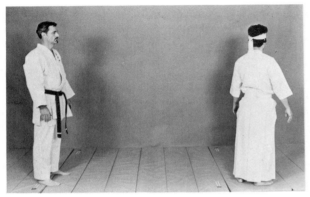

11-36

11-37

11-38

11-39

11-40

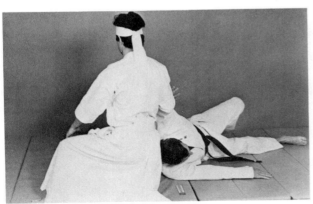

11-41

11-42

Technique 6: Hiki-Otoshi

Participants assume start position *(photo 11-43)*. Uke (man on right in photos) walks toward tori, his right hand in front, directed toward tori's shoulder *(photo 11-44)*. Tori pivots a quarter-turn, seizes uke's right wrist with his left hand, and places the edge of his hand on uke's forearm *(photo 11-45)*. (*Note:* In some schools the right hand presses against the hollow of *uke's* elbow.)

Tori continues to backstep in a counterclockwise circle and lowers himself onto his left knee *(photo 11-46)*, throwing opponent *(photo 11-47)* off balance and to the mat *(photo 11-48)*. Uke assumes a sitting position *(photo 11-49)*, and both participants stand.

Technique 7: Kodaore

Participants assume start position *(photo 11-50)*. Both walk toward one another, and tori (man on right in photos) stops approximately three steps away, lifts his hand (in a knife-

hand position), and attempts a strike to uke's head *(photo 11-51)*. Uke dodges the attack by withdrawing backward and to his left, grasping tori's right hand with his right hand. Uke attempts a hip movement to throw tori *(photo 11-52)*, which tori blocks with his abdomen. Uke is now off-balance, which tori takes advantage of by dropping to his left knee and throwing tori across his right leg *(photo 11-53)* and onto the mat *(photo 11-54)*. Uke assumes a sitting position, and both participants rise to their feet.

11-43

11-44

11-45

11-46

11-47

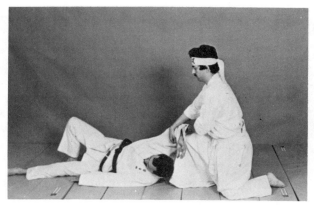

11-48

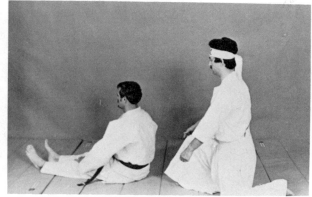

11-49

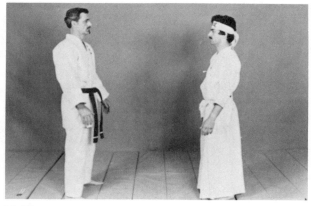

11-50

11-51

11-52

11-53

11-54

Technique 8: Uchi-Kudaki

Participants stand facing each other *(photo 11-55)* at a distance of 12 feet. Both advance toward each other with slow steps until tori (man on left in photos) is three steps away from uke. At this point tori raises his left hand in knifehand position as if to strike out at uke *(photo 11-56)*.

Uke grasps tori's attacking hand; steps in, putting his arm around tori's waist; and attempts a hip throw *(photo 11-57)*. Tori places his left hand on uke's waist and resists his movement by lowering his body and resisting with his abdomen by tightening his muscles and trying to stay rooted to the ground. Tori bends slightly backward, unbalancing uke to his left side. Tori takes several small steps backward *(photo 11-58)* and then suddenly drops to his right knee, throwing opponent over his left knee *(photo 11-59)* and to the mat *(photo 11-60)*. Uke assumes a sitting position

(photo 11-61), and both participants slowly stand.

Technique 9: Tani-Otoshi

Tori (man on left in photos) turns to face joshi while uke circles behind him *(photo 11-62)* about six feet away. Uke grasps tori from behind with a bias toward his left side *(photo 11-63)*. He then pushes on tori to force him to bend forward *(photo 11-64)*. Tori goes with the movement, bringing his chest parallel with the mat. He then jerks forward as if to attempt to throw the uke over his back. Uke naturally resists by pulling upward. When he does, tori goes with the movement, drawing himself erect *(photo 11-65)*, dropping down to his right knee, and throwing uke over his left knee *(photo 11-66)* to the mat *(photo 11-67)*. Uke assumes a sitting position *(photo 11-68)*, and both participants rise slowly to a standing position.

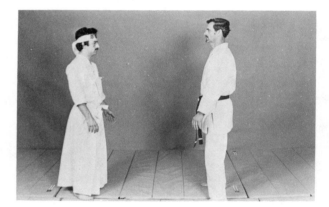

11-55

11-56

11-57

11-58

11-59

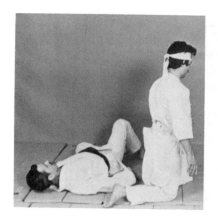

11-60

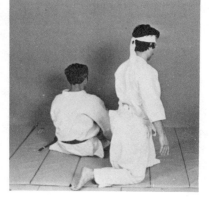

11-61

11-62

11-63

11-64

11-65

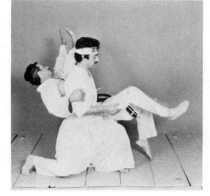

11-66

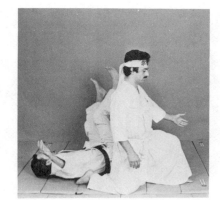

11-67

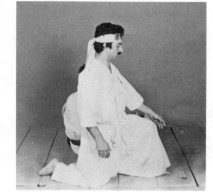

11-68

Technique 10: Kuruma-Daoshi

Participants begin in the same manner as for Technique 9 *(photo 11-69)*. Uke (man on right in photos), by grabbing tori from behind, tries to unbalance him to his left back by pushing his right shoulder with his right hand and pulling him by the left collar with his left hand *(photo 11-70)*. Tori goes with the movement but stays erect and ducks under his left armpit *(photo 11-71)*, and falling to the ground *(photo 11-72)*, executing a yoko-gu-ruma[40] *(photo 11-73)*, and taking the uke to the mat *(photo 11-74)*. Uke comes to a standing position while tori lies outstretched on mat for a few moments *(photo 11-75)*.

Technique 11: Shikoro-Dori

Participants assume a standing posture *(photo 11-76)*. Uke (man on left in photos) advances toward tori, grasping his belt. However, the grasping action is never secured by uke because tori steps to his right side and parries uke's hand, simultaneously grasping uke's chin with his left hand *(photo 11-77)*. Tori, by using head control, forces uke to turn around (by rotating his chin); at the same time tori brings his right hand to uke's chin *(photo 11-78)*. Tori drops to his left knee *(photo 11-79)*, throwing uke on his back *(photos 11-80 and 11-81)*. Uke assumes a sitting posture *(photo 11-82)*, and both slowly rise to a standing position. (*Note:* Some schools have tori, after turning uke with chin control, then grasp uke's shoulders to pull him down across upright right knee rather than retaining chin grip.)

11-69

11-70

11-71

11-72

11-73

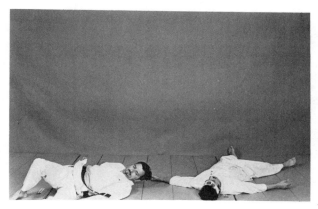

11-74

11-75

11-76

11-77

11-78

11-79

11-80

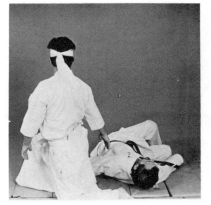

11-81

11-82

Technique 12: Shikoro-Gaeshi

Participants assume a start position facing each other *(photo 11-83)*. Uke (man on left in photos) follows the same procedure as in Technique 11, but this time he actually grasps tori's belt *(photo 11-84)*. Uke attempts to use his grip on tori's belt to lift him over his hip. Tori blocks this action by lowering himself and tightening his abdomen. At the same time, tori reaches over and turns uke's head clockwise *(photo 11-85)*. This action on uke's head unbalances him to right. Tori takes advantage of this by grasping his shoulders *(photo 11-86)* and sitting straight down *(photo 11-87)*, throwing uke over his extended right leg *(photo 11-88)*. (*Note:* In ancient days tori would have grasped the shoulder piece [*shikoro*] on uke's armor.) Uke assumes a sitting position *(photo 11-89)*, and both stay this way for a few seconds before rising slowly to a standing position.

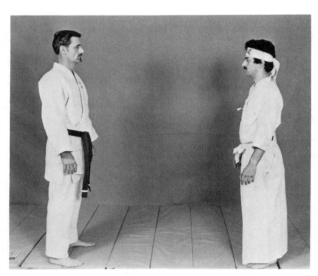

11-83

11-84

11-85

11-86

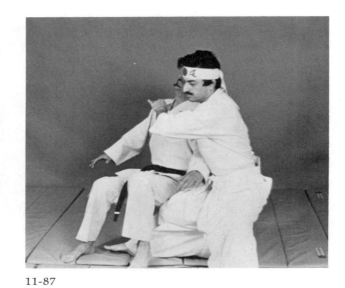

11-87

11-88

11-89

Technique 13: Yudachi

Participants stand facing each other in start position *(photo 11-90)*, about three feet apart. Tori (man on left in photos) seizes uke's lapels with both hands *(photo 11-91)*. Then tori, with the help of his left hand, seizes both lapels in his right hand. Uke advances forward and simultaneously grasps tori's left sleeve. Tori in turn grasps uke's right sleeve with his left hand. Both step to tori's rear, unbalancing uke forward. Immediately tori drops to his left knee *(photo 11-92)* and executes a uki-otoshi[60] throw *(photo 11-93)*, taking opponent to mat *(photo 11-94)*. Uke assumes a sitting posture on mat *(photo 11-95)*. Both participants pause a moment, then rise slowly to a standing position.

Technique 14: Taki-Otoshi

Both participants stand facing each other in start position *(photo 11-96)*, about three feet apart. Tori (man on right in photos) reaches out and grasps uke's lapel with his right hand *(photo 11-97)*. Uke then grasps tori's right sleeve with his left hand. Uke advances forward with his right foot and, passing his right arm around tori's waist (grasping at the belt), attempts to throw tori with a hip throw. Tori blocks action with his abdomen, grasps uke's belt with his left hand *(photo 11-98)*, and spins backward counterclockwise *(photo 11-99)*, throwing opponent with a yoko-wakare[61] technique *(photo 11-100)* and taking uke to mat *(11-101)*.

Uke immediately rolls to a standing position. Tori pauses, outstretched on mat, for a moment. Then both rise to a standing posture and return to original start positions at beginning of kata and execute a standing bow. This ends the first part of kata, omote.

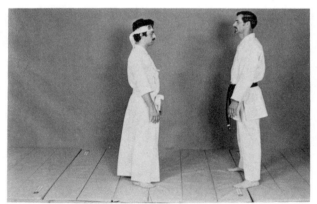

11-90

11-91

11-92

11-93

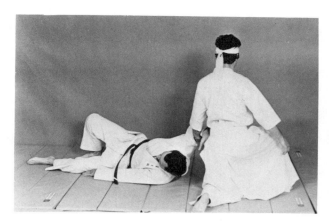

11-94

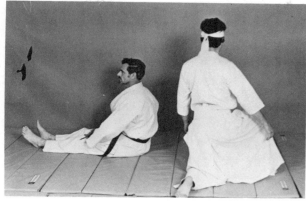

11-95

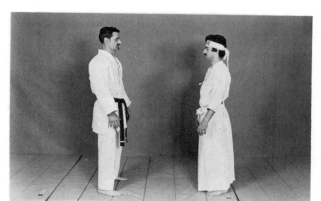

11-96

11-97

11-98

11-99

11-100

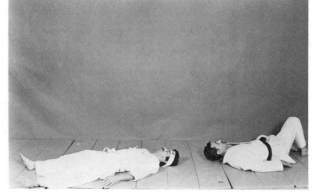

11-101

URA

All movements in the second part of this kata are done with smooth, *rapid* actions. Both attack and defense flow together without hesitation, quickly and cleanly.

There is absolutely *no* cause-and-effect relationship between one technique and the next. All seven actions of this kata flow together as one.

Technique 1: Mi-Kudaki

Participants bow again and approach each other in the center of demonstration area. Tori (man on left in photos) turns to face joshi, and uke approaches him from behind *(photo 11-102)*.

Uke grasps tori in the same manner as in Technique 1 (omote), grasping his belt and lifting his left leg. However, this time when the uke attempts to throw tori with hip action, tori grasps uke's left wrist with his right hand and slips his left arm under uke's left *(photo 11-103)*. Tori retains a grip on uke's arm, pivots counterclockwise *(photo 11-104)*, and falls to the ground *(photo 11-105)*, throwing uke on his back *(photo 11-106)*.

Technique 2: Kuruma-Gaeshi

Uke (man on left in photos) comes to a standing position after Technique 1, and tori immediately stands. Uke runs toward tori with his arms extended as if to grab him *(photo 11-107)*. Tori yields to the push, grasping uke's uniform under the armpits *(photo 11-108)* and falls back in the direction of uke's forward momentum. Uke is caught in the momentum and is thrown over tori *(photo 11-109)* to the mat behind tori's head *(photo 11-110)*.

Uke rolls to a standing position, and tori immediately gets up from the mat.

11-102

11-103

11-104

11-105

11-106

11-107

11-108

11-109

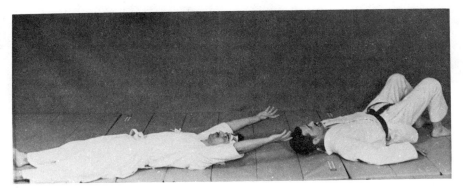

11-110

Technique 3: Mizu-Iri

Uke (man on left in photos) rushes at tori with left hand extended to grasp at tori *(photo 11-111)*. Tori seizes uke's gi (or wrist) and places his right hand under uke's left armpit *(photo 11-112)*. Tori pulls uke in the direction of his pushing momentum, at the same time falling to the ground and throwing uke over his (tori's) extended body *(photo 11-113)*. This throwing action, called yoko-wakare, takes uke to the mat *(photo 11-114)*, at which time he rolls to a standing position, and tori stands up rapidly.

Technique 4: Ryu-Setsu

Tori (man on left in photos) runs at uke, who has recovered from his last fall *(photo 11-115)*. Tori feints (kasumi) with his right hand (a waving action at uke's face that draws his attention to the action and away from tori's real intentions). This kasumi action forces uke to withdraw his head quickly, breaking his composure *(photo 11-116)*. Tori takes advantage of this by grasping uke *(photo 11-117)*, falling to the mat *(photo 11-118)*, and throwing uke over his body *(photo 11-119)* and to the mat *(photo 11-120)*. Uke rolls to standing position, and tori immediately returns to standing posture.

11-111

11-112

11-113

11-114

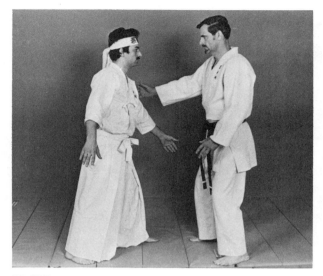

11-115

11-116

11-117

11-118

11-119

11-120

Technique 5: Saka-Otoshi

Uke (man on left in photos) rushes at tori with his left hand extended as if it were a dagger *(photo 11-121)*. Tori sidesteps the attack, grasps uke's arm *(photo 11-122)*, and throws him in the direction of his rushing momentum by dropping down on the right knee *(photo 11-123)* and pulling vigorously on uke's trapped arm *(photo 11-124)*. This action takes uke into the air and to the mat *(photo 11-125)*. Uke immediately comes to a standing position and faces tori.

Technique 6: Yuki-Ore

Uke (man on right in photos) rushes at tori, who is walking in front of him and facing joshi *(photo 11-126)*. Uke attempts a bear-hug action on tori by encircling his shoulders with his arms *(photo 11-127)*. Tori raises his arms to prevent this action, grasps uke's right arm *(photo 11-128)*, drops to his right knee, and executes a seoinage[16] throw *(photo 11-129)*, taking uke to the mat *(photo 11-130)*.

Uke immediately comes to a standing position.

11-121

11-122

11-123

11-124

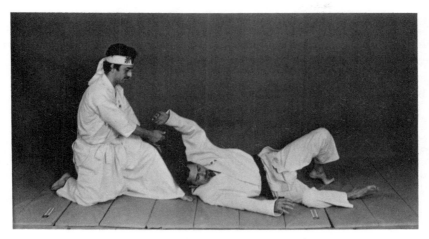

11-125

11-126

11-127

11-128

11-129

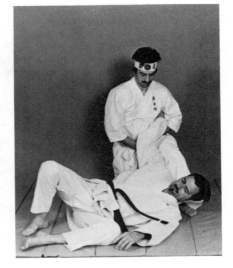

11-130

Technique 7: Iwa-Nami

At the moment that uke (man on right in photos) gets up and faces tori, tori performs a double feinting action (called *ryote-kasumi*) at uke's face with both hands *(photo 11-131)*. This feinting action forces uke to move his head backward, breaking his concentration and allowing tori to grasp his lapels *(photo 11-132)*. Tori then throws uke by pulling him to the ground as tori himself falls backward *(photo 11-133)*, forcing uke to fly over his body to the mat *(photo 11-134)*. Uke immediately rolls to standing posture as tori stands.

Ending Salutation

Both participants return to original start positions. They readjust their judogi (uniforms) and then turn to face joshi for a bow *(photo 11-135)*. They turn back toward each other and bow *(photo 11-136)*. This terminates the Koshiki-no-kata.

11-131

11-132

11-133

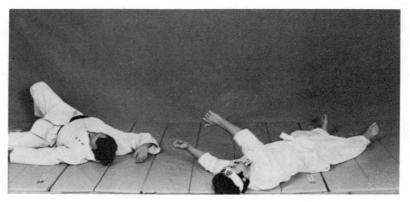

11-134

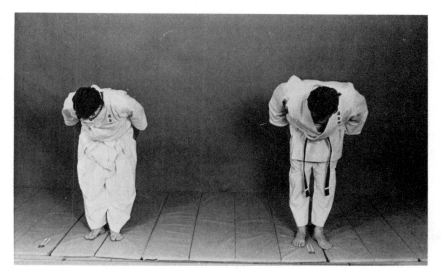

11-135

11-136

PART IV:
SELF-DEFENSE
TECHNIQUES

There is a misconception today
That judo is only a sport.
However, true advanced judo
Incorporates many methods of
Atemi (striking/kicking),
Which, when coupled with throws and
Other techniques,
Make judo perhaps the most
Realistic and effective means of self-defense
Available today!

12
ATEMI-WAZA
(STRIKING/KICKING TECHNIQUES)

Atemi-waza, or striking and kicking methods aimed at the body's vital areas or nerve centers, is perhaps the most neglected branch of judo today. This is due to the fact that striking is illegal in a match.

It is with the atemi-waza methods that judo becomes both a long- and short-range method of fighting, short-range being throwing/holding and long-range being striking/kicking.

The essence of atemi-waza is to generate momentum in the body and then transmit this via a particular striking/kicking tool. This momentum involves both weight and speed; the physical energy of a blow depends on both the weight of the attacking object and the speed it is moving at: speed (S) + mass (M) = power (P). Double the weight $(M \times 2)$, and you double the energy of the blow; but double the speed, and you multiply the energy times four.

The most frequently used method of generating momentum is to execute a rapid twist of the hips combined with the power of the arms and/or legs and delivered through one of the attacking tools to a vital area on the opponent's body.

There are three levels of speed that are practiced and developed through training in atemi-waza. The first kind of speed, or first level, is the *untrained* speed. It is kind of the wind-up-and-throw-it method in which there is really no concentration or focus on the point of impact.

The second level is to throw the technique with blinding speed. All of one's attention and power are generated in the delivery; however, the conscious effort to withdraw the punch/strike/kick is always there. It is not yet developed or instinctive.

The third and most advanced level of delivering atemi-waza is called the *whiplash* method. Here, full focus, speed, and concentration are developed to deliver the strike as well as to withdraw it with such speed that there is a crack to the technique and an audible sound like a snap.

These general rules for speed are applicable to both striking and kicking. Always remember never to lock the knee or elbow joint during the execution of an atemi technique. This locking, combined with the whiplash delivery method, can cause permanent damage to the joints. It is therefore wise to keep the elbow and knee slightly bent during the execution of the techniques that follow.

THE ATTACKING TOOLS AND METHODS OF DELIVERY

In atemi-waza, as in other martial arts like karate and kung fu, most parts of the body can be used as lethal weapons. To make these so-called weapons most effective, they are aimed and delivered to the vital areas, or nerve centers, of the human body. These points correspond to the points used in Chinese acupuncture or Japanese *shiatsu* massage. Each different school of jujutsu had its own secret chart of the human weaknesses, and these charts were guarded very closely. When you master atemi-waza you can deliver a technique and predict the amount of damage that will occur. The following is a chart used by the Tenshin-shin'yo-ryu jujutsu aiki-jutsu system. Since Dr. Kano himself studied and mastered this system, it is safe to assume that these areas were the original targets for judo atemi-waza. The following chart, compliments of the All-Japan Seibukan Martial Arts and Ways Association, is a beginner chart (more comprehensive knowledge of anatomy is required in advanced ranks).

VITAL POINTS

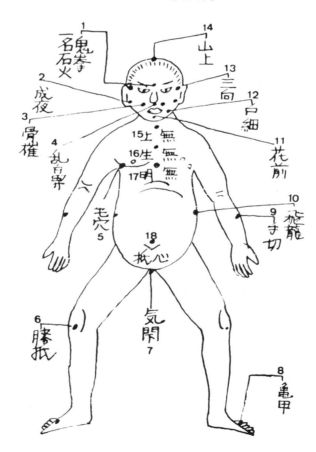

IMPACT KEY:

1—Moderate Pain
2—Sharp Pain
3—Severe Pain

4—Temporary Paralysis or Unconsciousness
5—Fatal Impact

GUIDE TO VITAL POINTS CHART ON PAGE 158

Number on Chart	English Name	Japanese Name	Location of Point	Best Attacking Tool	Result of Light Blow	Result of Medium Blow	Heavy/Full-Power Blow
1	Head center	*Uto*	Center of eyebrows	Forefist	2/3	4	5
2	Under ear	—	Indentation under ear	Extended knuckles	2	3	4
3	Cheekbone	—	Cheekbone under eye	Forefist, *shuto*	2	3	4 (impact can break bone)
4	Under nose	*Dokko*	Center under nose	Extended knuckles	2	3	4
5	Under arm	*Maeshun*	Armpit center	Elbow, foot edge	1	2	3
6	Knee	*Shitsu-kansetsu*	Knee joint	Foot edge	2	3	4 (with dislocation)
7	Groin	*Tsurigane*	Male reproductive organs	Knee, ball of foot	3	4	5
8	Instep	*Uchikurobushi*	Top of foot	Heel	2	3	4
9	Forearm	*Hini-kansetsu*	2½ inches below elbow	Knifehand	1	2	3
10	Side of body	*Get-sui'ei*	Last rib/floating rib	Fist edge	2	3	4
11	Chin	*Kachikake*	Center of chin	Forefist	2	3	4
12	Side of face	—	Center of cheek	Knifehand	1	2	3
13	Temple	*Kasumi*	Temple at side of head	Knifehand	3	4	5
14	Top of head	*Tendo*	Center of top of head	Fist edge, knifehand	2	3	4 (sometimes fatal)
15	Throat	*Hichu-do*	Center of throat	Forefist, knifehand, knuckles	3	4	5
16	Heart	*Kyototsu*	Center of chest	Forefist	2	3	4/5 (can stop heart)
17	Solar plexus	*Sui-getsu*	Opening under sternum	Forefist Straight: Upper motion:	2 3	3 4	4 5
18	Abdomen	*Myojo*	Stomach/intestine area	Ball of foot	1	2	3

STANCES

Before you can learn delivery of atemi-waza methods you must be able to stand correctly. Standing correctly involves proper distribution of weight in various positions or stances, called *dachi*. Various dachi have strong and weak points, and some are more applicable to certain situations than others.

Ready Stance
(*Musubi-Dachi*)

Concept: Weight is distributed equally on both feet (50/50). Feet are together at heels, with toes pointed away from one another (*photo 12-1*). When feet are completely together, another version of this stance, it is called *heisoku-dachi*.

Advantages: This is simply a ready stance and is not intended for fighting. A ready stance is a start position used before moving into a practical stance or is a transitory stance when one is shifting from one stance to another.

Open Ready Stance
(*Hachiji-Dachi*)

Concept: This is a more stable ready stance in which weight distribution is 50/50 and feet are shoulder width apart (*photo 12-2*).

Advantages: A light quick stance that allows moving in and out quickly. Stable side to side to limited degree.

Disadvantages: Weak in balance from front or back.

Horse Riding Stance *or* Horse Stance
(*Kiba-Dachi*)

Concept: A stance in which feet are two or three times shoulder width apart, toes pointed forward. Center of gravity is sunk close to ground. Back must be kept straight (*photo 12-3*).

Advantages: Extremely strong stance from side to side.

Disadvantages: Strong from front to back to a very limited degree, which is its major disadvantage.

Front Stance
(*Zen-Kutsu-Dachi*)

Concept: This is a very useful and the most practical stance in which to apply atemi techniques. Weight distribution is 70 percent on front leg and 30 percent on rear leg. Measured from toe to toe, feet are 1½ times shoulder width apart (*photo 12-4*).

Advantages: A very strong stance in which to deliver an atemi attack because it is so stable from front or back.

Disadvantages: Stance is slightly weaker from side to side.

Back Stance
(*Ko-Kutsu-Dachi*)

Concept: A very effective stance that is very stable from front or rear. Weight distribution is 60 percent on rear leg and 40 percent on front leg. Feet are placed 1½ times shoulder width apart with the rear leg bent as weight is placed predominately on it. Shoulders face forward with back straight (*photo 12-5*).

Advantages: A very effective stance to attack from while you are retreating or shifting your weight to the rear to prevent front assault.

Disadvantages: Stance is slightly more awkward than the front stance.

MAKING THE PROPER FIST

In judo, it is extremely important to learn how to make a proper fist so as to prevent injury to your hand when you strike out at somebody. Start with hand held open (*photo 12-6*). Roll fingers back, placing the fingertips tightly on the base of the fingers (*photo 12-7*). Close the fist up (*photo 12-8*) and tuck the thumb over the top of index finger (*photo 12-9*).

12-1

12-2

12-3

12-4

12-5

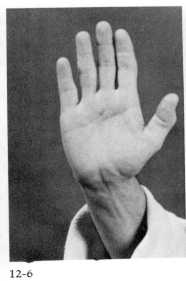

12-6

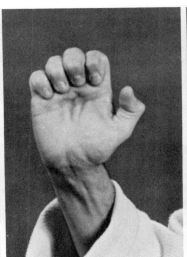

12-7

12-8

12-9

HAND TOOLS AND APPLICATIONS
Forefist (Seiken)

Impact Surface: (1) Main impact surface is the first two knuckles (index and middle) and finger surface (index/middle). This is called *seiken.* (2) Secondary striking surfaces include the back of the hand, called *ura-ken* and (3) the bottom of the fist, called *tettsui (photo 12-10).*

Applications:

Seiken: The straight punch can be delivered to a wide range of target areas. Here it is demonstrated attacking the face *(photo 12-11).* Note that the striking surface is only the first two knuckles.

Another method of using the seiken is to punch directly from the hips, driving the punch in an upward motion, as to the solar plexus *(photo 12-12).*

Ura-Ken: The back fist is seen here being aimed at the side of the face *(photo 12-13).* For maximum power, it is wise to extend the striking arm completely, leaving only a slight bend in the elbow for safety's sake.

Tettsui-Uchi: The fist edge, or hammer fist, is shown here being applied against the bridge of the nose *(photo 12-14).* This is a very powerful blow that can literally crush the nose. It is best applied in a downward action and should be used against nerve centers that afford this angle of execution.

Backhand (Haisho)

Impact Surface: Main impact surface of this hand weapon is the entire back of hand *(photo 12-15).* To form this tool, fingers should be kept tightly together with thumb bent and tucked over the index finger's knuckles.

Application: General delivery of this tool involves drawing the hand back *(photo 12-16)* and snapping out the technique *(photo 12-17).* In this case, the target area is the side of face.

Palm Heel (Teisho)

Impact Surface: Impact is delivered with the base of the inside of the hand, referred to as *palm heel (photo 12-18).* This is a very powerful tool that can be delivered in a downward, side, or rising action of the arm.

Application: The palm heel is best applied in the same manner as the fist edge (*tettsui*). Another effective use of this tool is the ear clap. When grasped by an opponent who is holding you firmly but still allows free use of your hands, deliver a simultaneous double palm heel strike to each ear of attacker—actually covering the entire ear when striking *(photo 12-19).* The excessive air pressure in the ear will cause severe pain or even unconsciousness.

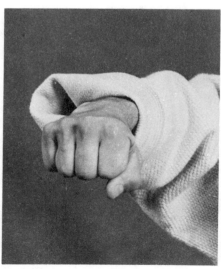

12-10

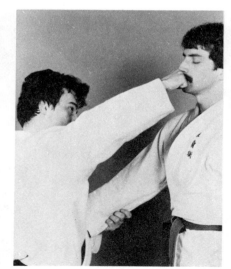

12-11

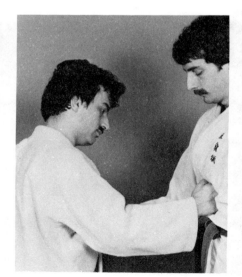

12-12

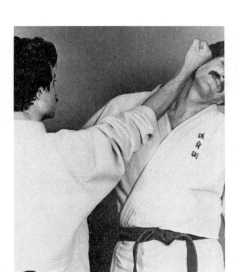

12-13

12-14

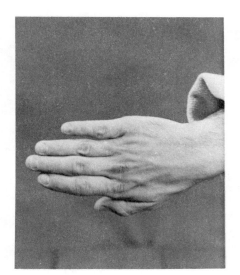

12-15

12-16

12-17

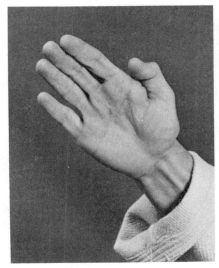

12-18

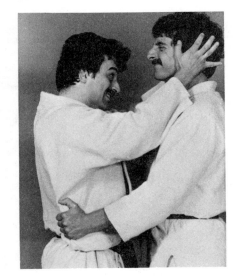

12-19

Knifehand (Shuto)

Impact Surface: The impact area on the knifehand is the edge of the palm near the little finger. To form this tool, hold all fingers tightly together and bend them slightly, causing tension in muscle at base of palm for added impact power. Tuck the thumb over index finger's knuckle *(photo 12-20)*. (*Note:* some judoka prefer to separate fingers slightly for greater muscle tension in edge of palm.)

Applications:

Inside Strike (uchi-shoto-uchi): This striking action draws the knifehand inward (toward your own body). To deliver this technique effectively, hold hand to the outside of your ear with open palm facing away from you *(photo 12-21)*. Draw the knifehand toward target, twisting it until the back of hand faces downward on impact *(photo 12-22)*. Remember also to twist the entire body through hip action to gain greater power. Target in this case is the opponent's temple. This is a *fatal* blow if delivered with full power.

Outside Strike (soto-shuto-uchi): A very powerful method of striking; execution is delivered in the same manner as illustrated for the backhand (haisho), except the tool is the knifehand *(photo 12-13)*. Target area illustrated is the side of neck. A heavy blow to this area will cause temporary loss of stability and coordination.

Downward Strike (omote-shuto-uchi): Again a very effective technique when delivered to nerve centers that allow this angle of attack. Execution is accomplished by holding the knifehand high over head and bringing it down powerfully on the target area, in this case the space under the nose (nerve center 4 on chart) *(photo 12-24)*.

Extended Middle Knuckle Fist (*Nakadate Ippon Ken*)

Impact surface. The extended portion of the middle knuckle is considered the impact surface. The tool is used by protruding the middle knuckle and securing it in place (to prevent collapse on impact) with the middle knuckles of the index and ring fingers *(photo 12-25)*.

Application: This particular tool is used in conjunction with a snapping action. In this example, the extended knuckles are applied against the floating ribs (nerve center 10 on chart) as opponent attempts to choke you *(photos 12-26 and 12-27)*. Impact with this technique will startle an opponent so you can follow up with other atemi techniques or a throwing/locking action.

Tiger's Mouth (Koko)

Impact surface: Area for contact is the *U* of the hand as formed by the index finger and thumb *(photo 12-28)*.

Application: This technique is applied almost exclusively in judo to the throat. After a straight impact (which alone can break the throat), the index finger and thumb act as a vise that can very literally tear out a human throat *(photo 12-29)*.

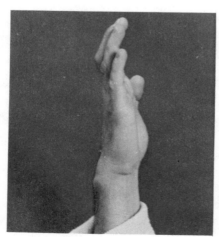

12-20

12-21

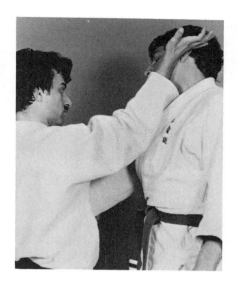

12-22

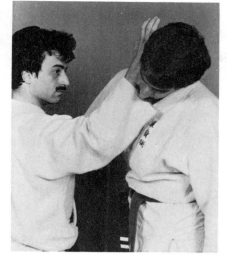

12-23

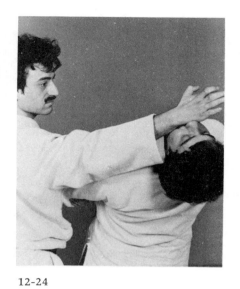

12-24

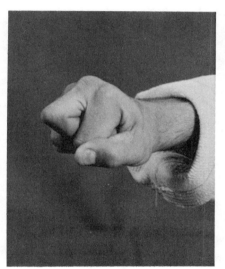

12-25

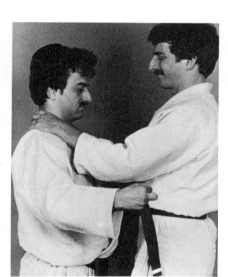

12-26

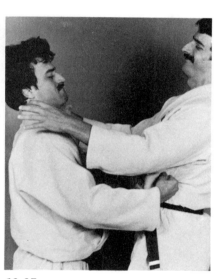

12-27

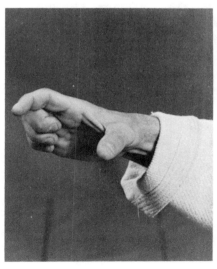

12-28

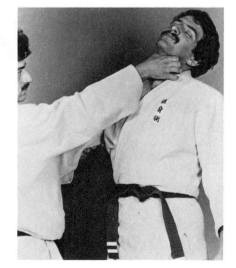

12-29

Fork Hand (Koko-Ken)

Impact surface: This technique uses the same striking surface as the preceding tool (koko), and it gains support from the knuckles of the other fingers *(photo 12-30)*.

Application: Like the preceding technique, the only target area for this tool used by the judoka is the throat. A heavy blow will shatter the larynx due to the extended knuckles. The index finger and thumb can then grip the throat and either tear it out or bring the opponent to submission *(photo 12-31)*.

Finger Jab (Nukite)

Impact surface: The tips of fingers of an extended hand are the striking surface. In reality, it is really only the tips of the index, middle, and ring fingers that come in contact with target. The tool is formed by extending the fingers and bending the palm inward to form a flat striking surface with these three fingers. The thumb is placed over the top of the index finger for support *(photo 12-32)*.

Application: The general targets for finger attacks are the soft vital areas of the body. In this case *(photo 12-33)*, the target area is the solar plexus.

Extended Finger (Ippon-Nukite)

Impact surface: The surface of impact is the tip of the index finger, which is supported for this impact by pressing hard against the middle finger (which is half bent and remains slightly bent) so as not to break on impact *(photo 12-34)*.

Application: Again, the vital areas that are attacked with this tool are the soft areas of the body. A favorite striking target for this particular tool is the eye. The attack is executed with a smooth, driving force that can cause total loss of eyesight for the attacker. This type of attack should be used only when one's life is threatened *(photo 12-35)*.

Two-Finger Attack (Nihon-Nukite)

Impact surface: Striking area includes the middle/ring/little finger, held close together; and the index finger. The three fingers and the one index finger act as two fingers attacking *(photo 12-36)*.

Application: Like all finger (nukite) weapons, the target areas for the two-finger attack are the soft vital areas, namely (and almost exclusively) the eyes *(photo 12-37)*.

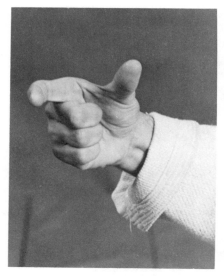

12-30

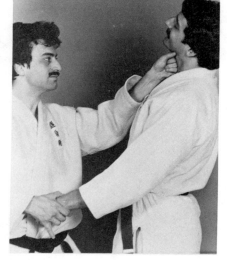

12-31

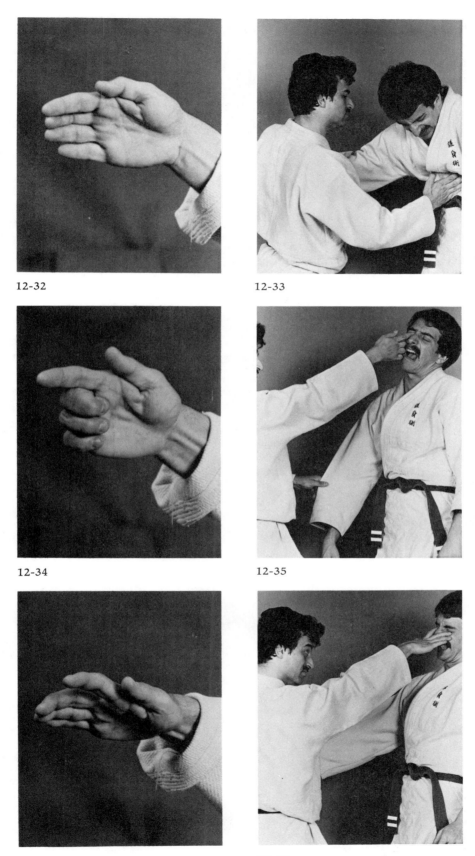

12-32

12-33

12-34

12-35

12-36

12-37

One-Knuckle Fist (Ippon-Ken)

Impact surface: The striking weapon is the middle joint of the index finger, supported by the bent thumb *(photo 12-38)*.

Application: Target areas for knuckle strikes *(ken-uchi)* are the same for the finger attacks (nukite), that is, the soft vital areas of the body. Target areas include temple, eyes, bridge of nose, and (as illustrated) the underside of the neck *(photo 12-39)*. Delivery of the attack is straight forward.

Ox Knuckle (Ayumi-Ken)

Impact surface: Impact area is the middle joint of the thumb as it is supported on the side of the fist *(photo 12-40)*.

Application: Same as for preceding technique. Delivery is usually in an arching motion created by the elbow's pulling the fist back in a circle and impacting target on the return motion. In this case, the opponent has been struck in the temple *(photo 12-41)*.

Forearm (Ude)

Impact surface: The inner or outer surface of the forearm is used for impact *(photo 12-42)*.
Applications:
*Inside Strike (*uchi-ude-uchi*):* Delivery of the forearm strike, in this case to the chin as opponent leans back, is delivered in an arching/snapping motion using the elbow to create a counterclockwise semicircle, *(photo 12-43)*.

Downward Strike (omote-ude-uchi): This is a crashing strike using the outside of the forearm. Delivery is accomplished by bending the arm at the elbow and lifting the bent arm up (with shoulder). Drive the forearm downward first with the shoulder and then with the straightening action of the elbow, *(photo 12-44)*.

Elbow (Empi)

Impact surface: The elbow is a unique tool because of its multiangle impact surfaces of front, middle, or bottom of elbow *(photo 12-45)*.

Applications: Delivery of the elbow strikes depends on the area of elbow used as the impact surface.

*Side Elbow Strike (*yoko-empi-uchi*):* Striking surface is the top or, as sometimes referred to, front portion of elbow. Direction of impact is straight forward. Target areas include face, abdomen, and (as illustrated) the solar plexus *(photo 12-46)*.

*Rising Elbow Strike (*age-empi-uchi*):* Striking surface is the middle of the elbow (the actual joint), and the attack is delivered in an upward action initiated by the shoulder joint *(photo 12-47)*.

Downward Elbow Strike (omote-empi-uchi): An extremely powerful elbow strike, the impact surface is the bottom of the elbow, and the target areas include face, kidneys, abdomen, and (as illustrated) the back of head *(photo 12-48)*.

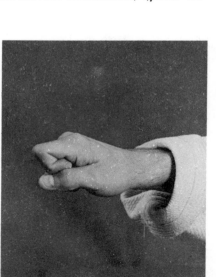

12-38

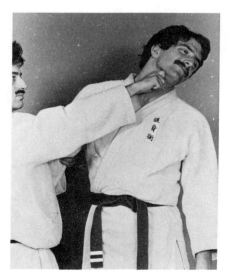

12-39

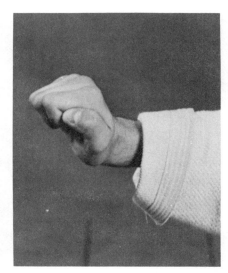

12-40

12-41

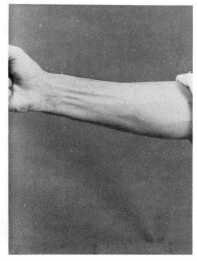

12-42

12-43

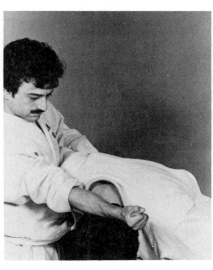

12-44

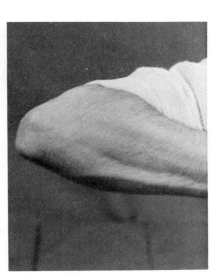

12-45

12-46

12-47

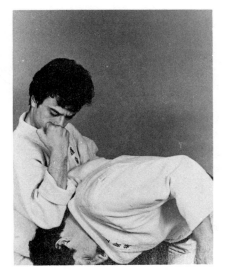

12-48

MISCELLANEOUS HAND WEAPONS

Full Extended Knuckles (Heraken)

In this case, all the foreknuckles of the hand are used to strike. Target areas include under nose, ribs, temple, and solar plexus (*photo 12-49*).

Ridge Hand (Haito)

Hand is formed the same as the knifehand (*shuto*), except the thumb is bent down to form a striking surface across index finger ridge and thumb ridge. Target areas include ribs, temple, ears, throat (*photo 12-50*).

Chicken Peak (Keiko)

Hand is formed by bunching all fingertips with the thumb. Striking surface is the fingertips. Attacks are delivered in a pecking motion to soft areas of the body like the eyes (*photo 12-51*).

KICKING METHODS AND FOOT TOOLS

Ball of Foot

Impact surface: The ball of the foot is formed by extending the ankle forward and curling the toes back (*photo 12-52*).

Applications:

Front Kick (mae-geri-kekomi): Kick is delivered by bringing the kicking foot up to the knee (*photo 12-53*) and thrusting foot forward, striking with the ball of the foot (*photo 12-54*). Kick is then brought back to knee and returned to ground.

Heel

Impact surface: The heel (*kakato*) is formed by drawing the ankle back (toward shins) and holding it in that position. Two surface tools are used: the back of heel (as in *ushiro-geri*), and the bottom of heel (as in *fumikomi*) (*photo 12-55*).

Applications:

Stamp Kick (fumi-komi): Leg is brought up to knee (*photo 12-56*), and the heel is brought straight down, in this case into opponent's head (*photo 12-57*). Leg is returned to knee and then to ground.

Rear Rising Kick (ushiro-geri-keage): This is a quick snapping kick that starts from the floor (*photo 12-58*) and is brought upward, driving the heel into opponent's groin (*photo 12-59*). Leg is then returned to ground. *Remember:* The kick is delivered with a *snap*, so kicking action and return to the ground should be lightning fast.

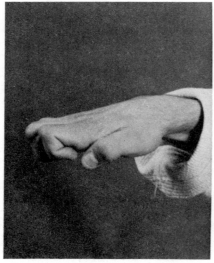

12-49

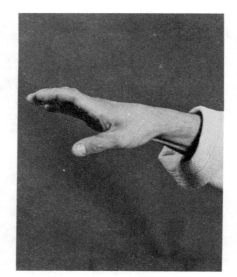

12-50

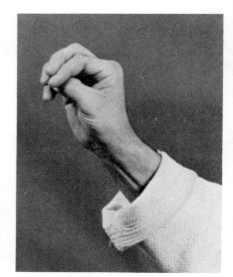

12-51

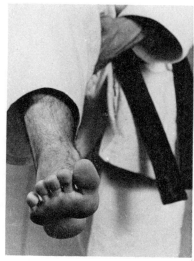

12-52

12-53

12-54

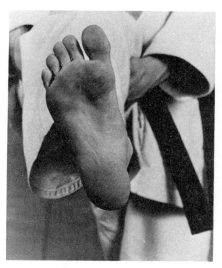

12-55

12-56

12-57

12-58

12-59

Edge of Foot

Impact surface: The impact surface consists of the entire area from the little toe to the heel at the edge of the foot. The toes are curled under and back for better surface control and protection (against toes being broken) *(photo 12-60)*.

Application:

Side Thrusting Kick (yoko-geri-kekomi*)*: A very effective and useful kicking method, especially against the shin or knee. Leg is brought up to knee as you show opponent your side *(photo 12-61)*. Kicking leg is brought straight down to kicking target (in this case the front of knee) with the edge of the foot *(photo 12-62)*. Kick is returned to knee and then brought to floor. (*Note:* This is a good kick to use if you want to dislocate an opponent's kneecap. The formula for delivery is to strike at a 45-degree angle with 65 pounds of pressure).

Knee

Impact surface: The knee itself is the impact surface after the joint has been bent (at least 45 degrees) *(photo 12-63)*.

Applications:

Roundhouse Knee Strike (mawashi-hiza-geri): Grasping opponent for support and pulling power, lift your rear knee *(photo 12-64)* and drive it with a semicircular motion (in this case counterclockwise) into opponent's abdomen *(photo 12-65)*. For added power, pull opponent into the strike by pulling toward you on his lapels.

Rising Knee Strike (age-hiza-geri): Again, grasping opponent for support and pulling power *(photo 12-66)*, lift rear leg off the ground and drive it forward and upward into the target area, in this case the groin *(photo 12-67)*. Remember to pull your opponent into the strike to add more power to it. (*Note:* Another variation on this kick is to grab opponent by hair and pull his head into the kick).

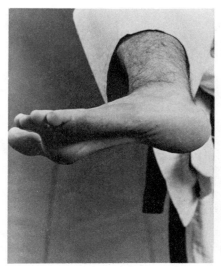

12-60

12-61

12-62

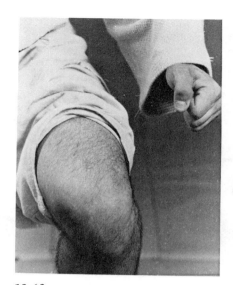

12-63

12-64

12-65

12-66

12-67

13
SELF-DEFENSE SEQUENCES AGAINST MODERN-DAY SITUATIONS

Up to this point, we have examined a number of individual techniques along with self-defense applications (found in the kata). In this chapter we will look at a few applications of judo for situations (and weapons) found in our modern-day society. It should be noted that, with the atemi-waza to weaken an opponent, any throwing technique in judo can be used in self-defense. To best put the techniques of judo to use on the street, the following points should be understood.

- *MA-AI (distance):* Ma-ai is the art of distancing yourself from your opponent. This is necessary for proper evasion and escape, blocking and countering. If you are closer to your opponent, it is easy to attack but more difficult to defend. If you are too far away, the reverse is true. It is best to stay in mushin-no-shin (see Chapter 2) to respond to the situation as called for through intuition.
- *KAMAE (posture):* In judo as it is applied for self-defense, the theory is not to maintain a stiff, rigid posture but instead to be relaxed and stable. From such a

posture you do not telegraph to your opponent your intentions to evade, block, or attack. Instead, you are telling him you are ready for whatever should come.
- *JU (yield):* The word *ju* means to move with or out of the direction of an attack or force. The idea is to use your opponent's strength and movement against himself. *Ju* also refers to the blocking of a strike in such a way that *less* strength is required to stop or control it.
- *AI (harmony):* Judo's use of the term *ai* is to be in tune with yourself and your situation during a confrontation. At first the stress is placed on physical harmony with your opponent's attack. The objective is to move with or control your opponent's strike at the very moment he threatens any movement to attack. Eventually, you become so in tune with an opponent's mind that just the thought of an attack puts you in control.
- *KI (concentrated energy):* Ki is a concentrated energy force accomplished through one-point mental and physical

concentration (see one-point meditation in Chapter 2). Later it becomes an inner strength, which is when this one-pointed (total) concentration practice is combined with breathing.[3]

- *MARUI (circular motion)/TENKAN (moving in a whirlwind fashion):* Correct evasion from an opponent's attack dissipates his energy in a circular fashion and then redirects his energy where *you* want it to overcome him. The reason one uses a circular dissipation (in contrast to linear dissipation, as in karate) is that there is no beginning and end; the defense leads into the counterattack without having to stop and start again.

With these concepts in mind we present the following modern-day sequences for common street attacks.

SEQUENCES

Club Defense
(or Attack with Baseball Bat)

1. Both face each other. The defender (man on right in photos) is in a relaxed but stable stance *(photo 13-1)*.

2. Opponent attempts an overhead strike. Do not block the attack but rather put up your hands, step to your left, and guide the club into a complete clockwise circle *(photo 13-2)*. Going with the circu-

13-1

13-2

lar momentum of the club, duck under opponent's armpit *(photos 13-3 and 13-4)* and throw the opponent over in a somersault *(photo 13-5)* to the ground *(photo 13-6)*.

3. Holding on to the hand with the weapon, deliver a stamping kick *(fumikomi)* to opponent's neck *(photo 13-7)*.

Downward Stab with Knife Defense

1. Defender (man on right in photos) faces opponent, who is readied with knife to stab him in overhead attack *(photo 13-8)*.

2. Following the *exact* concept that was laid out in the preceding club defense, allow the knife to pass by your right side and then use the momentum (clockwise) created by attacker's violent attempt to secure a V lock on opponent's attacking arm *(photos 13-9 and 13-10)*.

3. With attacker's arm securely locked behind him *(photo 13-11)*, push opponent to the ground, face first, and grasp his hair to better secure him in place *(photo 13-12)*. If opponent does not surrender, excessive upward pressure on his arm can break his shoulder.

13-3

13-4

13-5

13-6

13-7

13-8

13-9

13-10

13-11

13-12

Knife Defense against Straight Thrust

1. You face your opponent (man on left in photos), who is about to stab you with a straight thrust to your abdomen *(photo 13-13)*.
2. Block his thrusting attempt with the back of your forearm (if you are cut, there are no major blood vessels that can be severed in this part of the arm) *(photo 13-14)* and bring his arm in a large clockwise circle out of your way *(photo 13-15)*.
3. Before opponent can move his arm, secure it, trap it *(photo 13-16)*, and break the arm at the elbow *(photo 13-17)*.

Forward Slashing Knife Defense

1. Face your opponent (man on right in photos), who is about to slash at your face or throat *(photo 13-18)*.
2. Move out of the way of the slash *(photo 13-19)* and guide the opponent's arm safely to the side *(photo 13-20)*, securing a grip on his wrist.
3. Twist the attacker's wrist backward *(photo 13-21)*, forcing the opponent either to fall to the ground *(photo 13-22, 13-23)* or to suffer a separated wrist.

Note: This throwing technique is called *kote-gaeshi*.

13-13

13-14

13-15

13-16

13-17

13-18

13-19

13-20

13-21

13-22

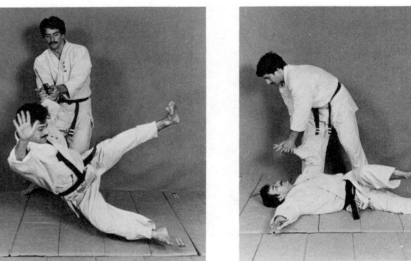

13-23

Backhand Slashing Knife Defense

1. You face your opponent (man on left in photos), who is going to attempt to slash you in a backhand fashion across your face *(photo 13-24)*.
2. As your opponent extends his arm to back-slash, catch his arm in your arms *(photo 13-25)* and break the opponent's arm at the elbow with pressure exerted from your left forearm *(photo 13-26)*.
3. Swing the opponent's arm in a clockwise circle *(photo 13-27)*, putting reverse pressure on attacker's shoulder as you trap the upper arm *(photo 13-28)*.
4. Dislocate opponent's shoulder by pulling up sharply as you twist in a clockwise circle. This action will throw him over *(photo 13-29)* and onto his back *(photo 13-30)*.

Backward Stabbing Knife Defense

1. Opponent (man on right in photos) is holding knife in a reverse grip and is attempting to stab you *(photo 13-31)*.
2. As he swings his body to stab, circle around in the direction of his stabbing force *(photo 13-32)* and catch his arm and head in a hara-gatame *(photo 13-33)*.
3. As opponent attempts to lift himself out of the hold, go with the lift, pulling sharply on opponent's neck and arm *(photo 13-34)*. Your options are either to stay in the hold until he surrenders or to pull up hard enough to break either his neck or arm.

13-24

13-25

13-26

13-27

13-28

13-29

13-30

13-31

13-32

13-33

13-34

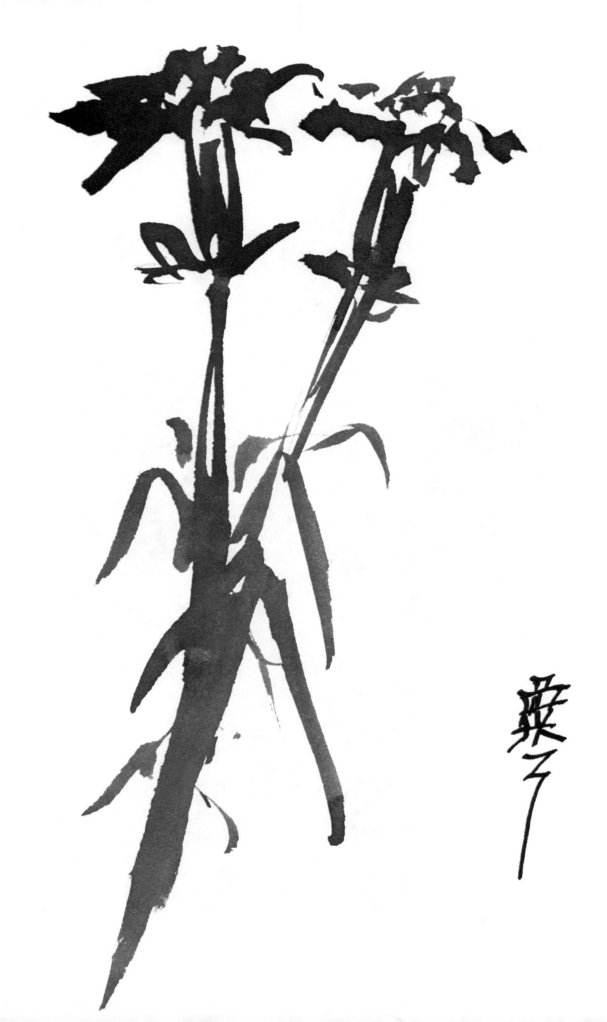

APPENDIX I:
TREATING AND PREVENTING INJURIES

The field of athletic injuries is a very specialized one; it would take a complete book to do it justice. In this appendix, I will mention only those injuries most common to judo and give suggestions for treatment and prevention. It is necessary to consult a trained physician before undergoing a judo training program as well as in the event of injury. These are only guidelines for your reference.

THE SHOULDER
DISLOCATION

Dislocation is a condition in which the bones of the shoulder separate. This is a severe injury; seek medical help immediately.

Treatment: Immobilize the injured part and adjacent joints by keeping the upper arm close to the body and limiting further movement. Ice and compression may be used if they help keep you comfortable. Transportation to emergency facility is now possible.

Prevention: This type of injury is very difficult to prevent and is common during practice of certain locking techniques. The best prevention is to go easy during practice and to surrender immediately when opponent secures a lock that could hurt the shoulder rather than seeing how long you can take it.

FRACTURE OF COLLARBONE

This is an extremely common injury during the practice of ne-waza in judo. There are two types of collarbone breaks: (1) a break in the clavicle due to a direct blow, or (2) a stress fracture, when you are locked in a certain position and brought down to the mat.

Treatment: Immediate medical attention is required.

Prevention: The best prevention is to be in excellent condition. Strength exercises (with weights) as well as flexibility exercises in the shoulder area (yoga) will keep this area strong. If collarbone is sore, avoid contact to it to prevent fracture.

BROKEN SHOULDER BONE

This is defined basically as a fracture of one

of the three bones that make up the shoulder (clavicle, scapula, humerus). These breaks are common when you fall incorrectly during a randori session.

Treatment: Apply the following first aid technique (remember the acronym *RICES*).

- *Rest.* Rest on the mat and relax.
- *Ice.* This should be applied to the affected area.
- *Compression.* In order to limit internal bleeding, apply a compression bandage directly to the injured area. Place ice over the first layer of elastic bandage wrap and put more compression elastic wrap over the ice. The ice, along with the compression caused by the elastic bandage, will limit the amount of internal bleeding.
- *Elevation.* Elevating the injured area will cause less circulation to it and hence limit further bleeding.
- *Stabilization.* This means that if an area is injured (in this case the shoulder), all other joints leading to the shoulder should be immobilized.

After the application of RICES, immediate medical attention is advised.

Prevention: See "Fracture of Collarbone."

THE UPPER ARM
TENNIS ELBOW

This is an irritation of the extensor tendon of the muscles of the forearm. It is brought about by too much conditioning too soon.

Treatment: Rest and ice treatment are the best thing for this type of injury. Excessive pain can be eased with the injection of hydrocortisone from a physician. For those judoka who prefer a more natural approach, a poultice of comfrey root to the area coupled with rest will help the injury.

Prevention: Proper training is the best prevention. *Gradual* training to build up and strengthen the joint, along with period of *rest*, will prevent this from occurring.

DISLOCATION OF ELBOW

Dislocation of the elbow happens sometimes when a judoka fails to surrender during an arm lock and his partner snaps his elbow by mistake.

Treatment: Immediate medical attention is required. Get to an emergency facility immediately.

Prevention: Again, the best prevention is to surrender when you feel pain from an arm lock rather than seeing how long you can take it.

THE WRIST

A wrist injury, common in judo, can be the result of an improper fall in which the uke reaches out for the mat. Or it can be a result of too much pressure being applied during the training of kote-waza (wrist locking techniques).

BROKEN WRIST

Treatment: Immediate medical attention is required to set and plaster joint.

Prevention: Possible preventive techniques are to wrap and slightly pad the wrist area before practice. Proper instruction in ukemi-waza (falling techniques) is required to prevent this injury.

WRIST SPRAINS

Treatment: Immediate rest of all wrist activities. Ice with moderate wrapping is helpful.

Prevention: Keep wrist wrapped with standard wrist braces used in wrestling and tennis.

THE HANDS
BLISTERS

Since the hands are used to grip the judogi, blisters can occur. Blisters are nothing more than points on the skin where friction is allowed to occur, causing a buildup of fluid beneath one or more layers of skin.

Treatment: Puncture the blister with a sterile pin and let fluid drain off. To get all fluid out, compress the outer layers of the blister. *Do not* tear or cut the thin layer of skin from the blister area. This will act as a cover to prevent infection. Cover the area with an adhesive strip after applying a disinfectant to prevent infection.

Prevention: Prevent formation of blisters by taping fingers/hand in areas of greatest friction.

SORE HANDS

This develops from repeated pounding on the hands or from excessive weight training (holding the equipment).

Treatment: Soak hand in ice water to prevent swelling. Elevate hand to minimize swelling and possible trauma in that area (from excessive impact, such as someone falling on hand during ne-waza).

Prevention: Tape hands before training or, in the case of weight training, wear weight training gloves.

DISLOCATED FINGERS

A very common injury in judo, this is usually the result of falling incorrectly, such as when someone falls on you or when the fingers get trapped in the judogi and then a move is executed and the trapped fingers are broken.

Treatment: Tape the broken finger to its neighboring (unbroken) finger for support. Seek medical attention for setting the finger and stabilizing.

Prevention: The best prevention is to use care and good technique in judo. Protective taping and wrapping can also be used.

PELVIS BONE

Injury to this area occurs when lifting a very heavy individual for a throw or from excessive impact from a throwing technique. The result is a slight fatigue or stress fracture, usually near the bottom of the bone near the symphysis.

Treatment: Rest and abstain from all further judo activity until medical attention can be given.

Prevention: Prevention of this type of fracture involves building up the lower muscles through weight training and flexibility exercises. Be sure always to fall correctly and distribute your weight evenly across your body.

THE GROIN
BLOW TO THE TESTICLES

Any severe blow to this area can force the scrotum and immediate area to go into spasm—a very painful condition.

Treatment: Relief is brought on in the following ways.

1. Lie on your back and alternately bring each knee to your chest and then both knees.
2. Sit up on mat with legs extended. Have another judoka grab you from behind and lift you a few inches off the floor, then *drop* you to the mat on your buttocks. Repeat several times until pain is relieved.
3. Finally you may lie on your back and lift your leg off the floor, locking leg at knee. Have another judoka hold your leg and, with the bottom of his fist, deliver sharp blows to the heel of your foot in the direction of your head.

Prevention: Wear a supporter and/or protective cup.

GROIN PULLS

A groin pull is the stretching of the muscles of the groin. The cause is a sudden stretching of the muscles. This can happen if your leg is lifted up off the mat sharply (and high) or you attempt (or another judoka attempts) an uchi-mata-type throw.

Treatment: Apply RICES (see "Broken Shoulder Bone") method of muscle first aid. Apply this for a few days and begin a program of light, but progressive, stretching exercises.

Prevention: Increased muscle strength as well as flexibility in this area can prevent such injuries from occurring. Also, be sure to warm up properly before doing judo to prevent injuries of this nature.

THE KNEE
DISLOCATION OF THE PATELLA

This is not a very common injury in judo circles, but it does happen. By definition, a kneecap (patella) is dislocated when it falls out of its regular alignment and is stationed laterally to its original position. This is a very painful condition.

Treatment: Reduce the dislocation as quickly as possible (through RICES). An experienced sensei (teacher) should be able to slide the kneecap back to its midway position, and rest and RICES will allow you to heal yourself. If in doubt, consult your physician.

Prevention: The best prevention is to wear good-quality knee pads that protect the knee from the front as well as side to side. They should allow freedom of movement.

LIGAMENT INJURIES

There are *many* ligaments in the knee that can be injured by falling on the knee as well as from executing techniques incorrectly.

Treatment: RICES should be applied immediately. Immediate medical attention is required.

Prevention: Follow same preventive measures as for preceding condition. Also, attempt to strengthen and make flexible the muscles of the knee through weight training and yoga.

CARTILAGE PROBLEMS

Another common knee injury is damage to the cartilage in the form of tearing, compression, or wearing away.

Treatment: Evaluation of this injury by a trained physician is necessary. Also, herbalism (Chinese) and acupuncture have had great success in correcting this type of injury. I suggest you try these alternatives before consenting to any surgery.

Prevention: Padding, wrapping, taping, and otherwise protecting the joint from impact will lessen the chances of such a major injury.

OVERUSE PROBLEMS

Anytime the knee is used excessively there may be extreme (sharp) pain in the joint. This can be a chronic or just occasional problem. Regardless of the frequency, ignoring the pain can result in more serious problems in the future.

Treatment: Cessation of all judo activity is

the only way to help this injury. Many judoka, in addition to resting, apply herbal liniments. A source for such liniments is The Oriental Herb Co., 1744 West Devon Ave, Chicago, IL 60660.

Prevention: This is usually a condition found in beginners and not experienced judoka, whose bodies have become built up for judo activities. Beginners should keep in mind that they should build themselves up slowly rather than abuse themselves with excessive training at early stages.

THE LOWER LEG
ACHILLES TENDINITIS

This is a painful swelling of the area around the Achilles tendon. This tendon is the strongest in the body, but it does not have the synovial sheath that surrounds most tendons. This sheath is a double-layered tube through which the tendon passes, and it serves to lubricate and protect the tendon. This injury is caused by running too much (for conditioning) and by some types of weight training exercises.

Treatment: RICES is recommended for a few days, followed by gentle stretching of the area. Antiinflammatory herbal liniments may be used.

Prevention: Use weight training to strengthen the general area.

ACHILLES TENDON RUPTURE

In this case, the tendon is partially or completely ruptured (torn). When this happens no movement of the foot is possible.

Treatment: Immediate medical treatment and surgery are necessary.

Prevention: Warm up before involving yourself in judo. This type of injury is common in *shiai* (contests) in which someone pushes off against the mat with a foot, and it becomes twisted and the tendon tears. Proper application of judo techniques is another way of preventing this injury.

ANKLE SPRAINS

This is *the* most common judo injury. It can be the result of falling incorrectly, applying a judo technique incorrectly, or twisting your ankle on the mat during competitive drills. The problem with this injury is that it is often dismissed as a minor ankle pain when it could be more serious. Ankle sprains are ligament injuries; ankle strains are muscle injuries. Strains can heal themselves; sprains often require medical treatment. There are three degrees of sprains, the first being only a minor ligament sprain with the third being a total rupture.

Treatment: RICES should be applied within the first few seconds of the injury with judo activity ceasing. Complete rest of the ankle for 48 hours should then be followed by limited ankle stretching and activity. If the ankle is feeling stronger, continue RICES treatment with stretching. You may also use herbal liniments with a comfrey root compress. If swelling is still severe, medical treatment will be necessary.

Prevention: Strengthen the muscles in this general area. You can also wrap the ankle prior to workouts.

BRUISED HEELS

This is another common judo injury and is the result of falling onto a hard surface. Often, it happens when a part of the judoka's foot (usually the heel) falls off the mat and is bruised.

Treatment: See "Achilles Tendinitis."

Prevention: This injury is difficult to prevent. The only word of advice is to watch where you are being thrown and *stay on the mats.*

PREDISPOSING FACTORS FOR INJURIES IN JUDO

OVERTRAINING

Judoka who spend too much time in a given session, or over several consecutive days, are very prone to overuse or chronic types of injury. This usually happens when you have been inactive for a few weeks and then try to make it up by going all out the next few workouts. Prevent this type of injury by taking it easy and building up your stamina rather than trying to do it overnight.

POOR TRAINING

This is defined as increasing the intensity and types of workouts at an ever accelerating rate. The judoka attempts too much with too great an intensity too soon. This results in overuse-type injuries, which can be avoided by building the intensity of your workouts gradually.

STRUCTURAL ABNORMALITY

This is many times a genetic trait: high arches, poor posture, weak spine, one leg longer than the other, etc. Judo can still be performed with these abnormalities if the judoka keeps his limitations in mind and works around them. Not doing this can result in injuries that can prevent judo training for life.

LACK OF FLEXIBILITY

This is another big cause of injuries. Always involve yoga exercises in your workouts for better flexibility and integration of mind and body.

POOR TECHNIQUE

This can be your fault or the fault of your partner. This is an injury caused by negligence and can be prevented by being sure you are following textbook form. Remember, poor techniques are a ticket to major injuries.

APPENDIX II:
THE KODOKAN EMBLEM

Dr. Kano established the *Kodokan* as the main headquarters (*hombu*) for judo and as a place in which jujutsu and other martial arts systems could be practiced. It is said that there were facilities at the Kodokan to accommodate other ryu (schools) of bugei (martial arts). Today, however, the Kodokan has begun to concentrate its activities only on promoting judo around the world.

The first Kodokan was established in 1882 at the Eisho-ji monastery. It was a very small facility that Kano soon outgrew. Today, the Kodokan is a massively complex facility with many training areas (see Chapter 1 for more details). *Kodokan* means "a place to study the way." Naturally when Kano was considering an emblem to represent his new system and school it was important to represent this "way" (*do*) concept properly. He chose the Kodokan emblem because it represents the true meaning of judo as a personal way and as a way the nation could be proud of.

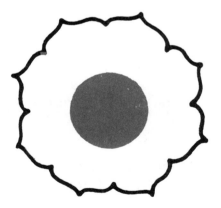

The emblem itself is comprised of two main things: the *sakura* and the rising sun.

The sakura is the cherry blossom. The cherry blossom is important because it represents and is the symbol for the code of *bushido* or the chivalry code of the samurai. Similar to the European code of chivalry, bushido was an intricate unwritten code of ethics believed to have been formulated by a samurai, Yoko

Yamagei. Bushido is believed to have grown out of a fusion between Buddhism and Shintoism. This fusion brought about seven principles:

1. Right Decision (*gi*). One must be able to make the right decision in the face of death, in battle, and in everyday situations. It must be a decision based on truth attained through unbiased evaluation.
2. Bravery (*yu*). The samurai was expected to be brave in battle. He was to give his life in a moment for the good of the cause.
3. Benevolence (*jin*). Without compassion and understanding, the samurai was nothing more than a trained killer. Universal love for all mankind is the key to bushido.
4. Right Action (*rei*). This refers to the correct *reishiki*, etiquette, in a given situation. The samurai believed it was better to lose one's life than be impolite.
5. Sincerity (*makoto*). Sincerity based on truth of heart and of action makes a man stand apart from another.
6. Honor (*melyo*). Glory without ego.
7. Loyality (*chugo*). Devotion to one's lord or teacher.

Kano wished to preserve the concepts of bushido, making them spiritual guidelines for all judoka. Inside the cherry blossom (sakura) is the rising sun. The fact that the sakura surrounds the sun may be Kano's way of saying that a strong Japan requires the concept of bushido for its true inner strengths.

The Kodokan emblem is the representative symbol for judo recognized around the world.

APPENDIX III:
BELT REQUIREMENTS

In my first book, I presented the time requirements with ages based on requirements set forth by the United States Judo Federation and United States Judo Association.[62] Most books on judo today give the sport requirements of either the USJA or the USJF. Since classical Kodokan judo contains traditional, sport and self-defense requirements, I have decided to present the standing requirements with time requirements for classical judo as endorsed by the Dai-Nippon Seibukan Budo/Bugei-Kai (All-Japan Seibukan Martial Arts and Ways Association). These requirements are also followed by the American Society of Classical Judoka.

HACHI-KYU—EIGHTH-LEVEL LOW RANK

Color of belt: White.

Time requirement: One must stay at this rank for at least two months before one is allowed to test for *shichi-kyu*.

Requirements: Basic belt worn by all beginners.

190

SHICHI-KYU—SEVENTH-LEVEL LOW RANK

Color of belt: Yellow.

Time requirement: Two months on white belt (*hachi-kyu*) is minimum time requirement.

Requirements:

1. Ukemi-waza (breakfalls): (a) Ability to fall in all directions—back (squat/sit/standing), side (sit/squat/standing), front (kneeling/standing), side rolling (squat/standing), raised back breakfall (squat), and protective somersaults; and (b) ability to be thrown and not get hurt.
2. Nage-waza (throwing): O-goshi (with variations of goshi, jigotai-goshi), o-soto-geri, tai-otoshi, and de-ashi-barai.
3. Katame-waza (ground work): Kesa gatame and kata gatame.
4. Yoga: Basic posture examination.
5. Terminology: Counting, commands, techniques.
6. Theory: Unbalancing, concept of throwing, stepping, gripping, standing.
7. Concept of Zen.
8. History of judo.

ROKU-KYU—SIXTH-LEVEL LOW RANK

Color of belt: Orange.

Time requirement: Four months minimum required at yellow (*shichi-kyu*).

Requirements: (in addition to all previous requirements, the following must be demonstrated):

1. Ukemi-waza (breakfalls): Back (leaping), side (leaping), front (leaping), side rolling (leaping), raised back breakfall (leaping); basic rolling over one obstacle.
2. Nage-waza (throwing): Uki-goshi, o-uchi-gari (2), ko-soto-geri, ko-uchi-geri, koshi-guruma, kata-guruma, sukui-nage, tsuri-komi-goshi.
3. Katame-waza (ground work): Kami-shiho-gatame, kuzure kami-shiho gatame, yoko-shiho-gatame, ude-gatame.
4. Randori (competition): Controlled randori; concept and ability.
5. Yoga: Improvement over last rank with more postures.
6. Terminology: Good command.
7. Theory: Use of force.
8. Zen: History with greater understanding from previous rank.
9. History of judo: More involved than previous rank.

GOKYU—FIFTH-LEVEL LOW RANK

Color of belt: Green belt. The end of the belt (on both ends) should have a white (or brown) stripe going around both ends.

Time requirement: One must have been an orange belt (*roku-kyu*) for a minimum of six months.

Requirements: (in addition to all previous knowledge and requirements, the following must be demonstrated):

1. Ukemi-waza (breakfalls): Advanced leaping over a single obstacle on to side, front, and back.
2. Nage-waza: Ippon seoinage, seoinage, hiza-guruma, sasae-tsuri-komi-ashi, ko-soto-gake, tomoe-nage.
3. Katame-waza (ground work): Tate-shiho-gatame, kuzure-tate-shiho-

gatame.
4. Creative throwing combinations.
5. Terminology: Complete.
6. Theory: Parts of a throw.
7. Zen: Concept of no-mind (mushin).
8. History of judo: Greater than previous ranks.
9. Ability to use judo in oncoming aggressive attacks.

YONKYU—FOURTH-LEVEL LOW RANK

Color of belt: Green belt. The end of the belt (both ends) should have two white (or brown) stripes going around both ends (four stripes total on belt).

Time requirement: Six months minimum required on green belt–first stripe (*gokyu*)before one can test for rank.

Requirements: (in addition to all previous requirements, the following must be demonstrated):

1. Ukemi-waza (breakfalls): Ability to roll over several people of various heights at one time.
2. Nage-waza (throwing techniques): Morote-geri, kochiji-taoshi, ko-tsuri-goshi, o-tsuri-goshi, harai-goshi, uki-goshi (variation), sumi-gaeshi, o-soto-guruma (three kinds).
3. Katame-waza (ground work): Juji-gatame, okuri-eri-jime.
4. Kodokan combinations (teacher's selection).
5. Creative combinations.
6. Randori: Controlled (one-point in contest requirement); sound contest skills and strategy.
7. Yoga: A command of postures with meaning and benefits.
8. Theory: All physical judo theory.

SANKYU—THIRD-LEVEL LOW RANK

Color of belt: Brown belt with one stripe on both ends (white or black stripes only).

Time requirement: Minimum of six months of green belt second stripe (*yonkyu*).

Requirements: (in addition to all other previous requirements, the following must be demonstrated):

1. Ukemi-waza (breakfalls): The ability to *leap* over (without hands touching) several people at various heights. Ability to be thrown and execute all ukemi-waza off the mat on any surface.
2. Nage-waza (throwing): Seoi-otoshi, o-soto-otoshi, uchi-mata, okuri-ashi-barai, yoko-guruma, yoko-otoshi.
3. Katame-waza (ground work): Ude-ga-rami, ashi-garami, kata-ha-jime, gyaku-jime, ude gatame, kata-juji-jime, gyaku-juji-jime, kuzure kata-juji-jime.
4. Randori: Controlled (two-point in contest requirement); good contest skills with good strategy.
5. Yoga: Greater knowledge than previous rank.
6. Yoga pranayama: Concept and knowledge with demonstration.
7. Concept and knowledge of meditation.
8. Philosophy: Judo's Three Cultured Principles along with judo's Three Philosophical Principles.
9. Zen: Detailed history.
10. Ability to apply judo in self-defense situations.

NIKYU—SECOND-LEVEL LOW RANK

Color of belt: Brown with two white or black stripes on each end.

Time requirement: Minimum of six months on brown belt first stripe (*sankyu*) before one can test for nikyu.

Requirements: (in addition to all previous requirements, the following techniques must be demonstrated):

1. Nage-waza (throwing techniques): Ashi-guruma, hane-goshi, harai-tsuri-komi-ashi, tani-otoshi, hane-maki-komi, utsuri-goshi, o-guruma, soto-maki-komi, uki-otoshi, uki-waza, yoko-wakare, ushiro-goshi, ura-nage, sumi-otoshi, and yoko gake.
2. Katame-waza (ground work): Kuzure ude-garami, kuzure ude-gatame (two of

them), kuzure juji-gatame, hiza gatame, kuzure hiza gatame, hadaka jime, kuzure hadaka-jime, kuzure kata-ha-jime (two of them).
3. Kodokan combinations (all).
4. Creative combinations.
5. Randori: Exceptional strategic accomplishment for rank.
6. Yoga: Greater knowledge than previous rank.
7. Kata: The history and philosophy behind kata.
8. History of judo: Complete.
9. Philosophy of judo: Complete.

IK-KYU—FIRST-LEVEL LOW RANK

Color of belt: Brown with three white or black stripes on each belt end.

Time requirement: Minimum of six months on brown belt second stripe (*nikyu*). For exceptional judoka who compete often and earn high scores, a minimum of three months is acceptable.

Requirements:

1. Nage-waza (throwing): Te-guruma, ude-garami-nage, kakato-gaeshi, eri-seoinage, kuki-nage, hiji-otoshi, yama-arashi, harai-makikomi, seoi-hane-go-shi, uchi-makikomi, o-soto-maki-komi, kani-basami, tawara-gaeshi, hiji-taoshi.
2. Katame-waza (ground work): Kote-waza, ashi-kansetsu-waza, sekizuki-waza, and countering techniques to all osae-komi with a complete command of ne-waza strategy.
3. Zen: Detailed philosophy.
4. Yoga: Greater physical knowledge/ability and command of philosophy.
5. Randori: Ability to apply concepts learned in contests.
6. Jujutsu: Defense against wrist grabs, body grabs, chokes, punching, pushing, hand squeezes, clubs.

SHODAN—FIRST-LEVEL ADVANCED RANK

Color of belt: Black with one white (or red or gold) stripe at each end.

Time requirement: A minimum of six months on brown belt third stripe (sankyu). At least 3–3½ years (depending on whether one has a regional/national competition status) are required in *kyu* (low ranks) before one can test. The test must be conducted before a board of three black belts, and this must be initiated by *Seibukan* and not applicant (in other words, he is told when he can test; he cannot ask).

Requirements: (in addition to all other requirements so far, the following must be demonstrated):

1. Nage-waza (throwing): Ability to apply all throws in combination with each other and with hold-downs.
2. Yoga: One must test simultaneously for a teaching license in yoga.
3. First aid: Complete and total command of first aid skills for dojo injuries along with *katsu* and *kappo* first aid.
4. Kata: *Nage-no-kata, Katame-no-kata, Gon-osen-no-kata.*
5. Endurance: Must be in excellent condition (muscular/skeletal and cardiovascular).
6. Atemi-waza: Command of striking/kicking techniques used in judo.
7. Jujutsu: Defenses against knife, gun, club, and multiple attackers.

NIDAN—SECOND LEVEL ADVANCED RANK

Color of Belt: Black with two stripes of white, red, or gold on each belt end.
Time Requirement: At least 1½ years as a first-degree black belt is required.
Requirements: (in addition to all other requirements to date, the following must be demonstrated):

1. Atemi-waza: Greater dexterity and control in all striking, punching, and kicking methods. Complete knowledge of all 175 body nerve centers (with impact variability knowledge).
2. Kata: Ju-no-kata, Kime-no-kata, and Kodokan Goshin-jutsu.
3. Jujutsu: Greater dexterity and more knowledge in each self-defense situation.

SANDAN—THIRD-LEVEL ADVANCED RANK

Color of belt: Black with three stripes of white, red, or gold on each belt end.
Time requirement: Minimum of two years as a second-degree black belt (*nidan*).
Requirements:

1. Kata: Itsutsu-no-kata, Seiryoku-zenyo kokumin-taiiku, Kime-shiki.
2. Jujutsu: Command of basics and foundations of Kito-ryu jujutsu.

Again, in testing, all requirements from all kyu and dan ranks must be demonstrated.

YONDAN—FOURTH-LEVEL ADVANCED RANK

Color of belt: Black with four white, red, or gold stripes at each belt end.
Time requirement: At least two years as a third-degree black belt (*sandan*).
Requirements:

1. Kata: Koshiki-no-kata, Renkoho-no-kata.
2. Jujutsu: Ability to attain the rank of oku-eri in Kito-ryu jujutsu. Preliminary ability in Tenshin-shin'yo-ryu aiki-jujutsu.

GODAN—FIFTH-LEVEL ADVANCED RANK

Color of belt: Black with five white, red, or gold stripes at each belt end.
Time requirement: At least four years required on fourth-degree black belt (*yondan*).
Requirements:

1. Kata: Shobu-no-kata and Go-no-kata.
2. Jujutsu: Ability to receive a rank of oku-eri in Tenshin-shin'yo-ryu aiki-jujutsu.

Exceptional dedication and knowledge required for awarding of this rank. Contest skills are no longer required at godan. Instead, one studies the methods of judo's past in an attempt to protect this knowledge from extinction.

ROKUDAN—SIXTH-LEVEL ADVANCED RANK AND SHICHIDAN—SEVENTH-LEVEL ADVANCED RANK AND HACHIDAN—EIGHTH-LEVEL ADVANCED RANK

Color of belt: Black with appropriate number of stripes or a red and white patched belt.

Time requirement: A minimum of 10 years required between each of these ranks. In exceptional cases, the minimum time has been lowered to five years. Never shorter.

Requirements: The major requirement is the promotional value and dedication one has for judo. Has he promoted the art on a national level? An international level? Has he gone beyond technique to the more spiritual realm? These are important considerations in being considered for these ranks. In addition, the study of *jodo* (staff art) and *iai-do* (sword art) is required for these ranks.

A few notes to keep in mind when reviewing these qualifications:

1. Up to *nidan* (second-degree black belt), the requirements can be shifted slightly at the teacher's option. As long as they accumulate correctly by *shodan* and *nidan* it is permissible. These are general guidelines for the sensei.
2. These are the classical requirements for the Dai-Nippon Seibukan Budo/Bugei-Kai and the American Society of Classical Judoka. Those who are ranked under USJA or USJF will find many classical requirements involving the traditional bugei that they are not familiar with. This is because the classical organizations are attempting to preserve the bugei forms from extinction and have incorporated them into judo rank. These requirements are in the higher dan ranks so as to keep *shodan* requirements pretty much standard in judo (again, there are exceptions).
3. Minimum age: Follow the minimum age chart from my first book, *The Complete Book of Judo.*[63]

4. *Kudan* (ninth-degree) and *judan* (tenth-degree) are determined individually and requirements are not standard. Although there are a few *kudans*, there are no living *judans*. Both these ranks have the option of wearing a solid red belt instead of a black one.

INSTRUCTOR CERTIFICATION

Note: Both the All-Japan Seibukan Martial Arts and Ways Association and the American Society of Classical Judoka have different qualifications and different names for their licenses. They are listed separately below.

SENIOR INSTRUCTOR LICENSE

Organization: American Society of Classical Judoka.

Rank: One must have a minimum of a *shodan* rank.

Purpose: This license is issued to give one the authority to issue rank. Each license is issued on an individual basis. Usually a *shodan* is allowed to issue rank up to ik-kyu. However, one must be at least a *sandan* before one is licensed to give a *shodan* rank.

Requirements:

1. Apprenticeship under a senior instructor for one year.
2. Extensive first aid training.
3. Proven ability to teach.
4. A thesis must be submitted on a topic approved by ASCJ.
5. Referee training—apprenticeship for six months under a senior instructor detailing only refereeing methods. This license allows one to officiate at ASCJ events.

CERTIFIED INTERNATIONAL INSTRUCTOR

Organization: All-Japan Seibukan Martial Arts and Ways Association.

Rank: One must have a minimum of a *shodan* rank.

Purpose: This license is issued to give one authority to issue rank. Each license is issued on an individual basis. Usually you are allowed to promote up to the rank under your present rank (for example, a *nidan* can promote up to a *shodan*). This license is recognized around the world and is recognized by the International Judo Federation (and Kodokan).

Requirements:

1. Apprenticeship for two years under a Certified International Instructor.
2. One must hold a Red Cross first aid training card.
3. One must prove his ability to teach by having personally trained (under supervision) a first-class student up to ik-kyu. This training is under the supervision of a Certified International Instructor (part

of the two-year apprenticeship in requirement 1).
4. One must have a total and complete knowledge of judo—its techniques, history, and philosophy—and knowledge of Zen and yoga (with instructor's certificate in yoga).
5. A thesis (of no fewer than 50 pages) must be submitted by the applicant on a subject approved by Seibukan headquarters in Japan.
6. This license gives the holder the ability to officiate at national and international judo events. Therefore, a great command of the rules with supervised experience in officiating is required.

APPENDIX IV:
OPENING A DOJO SUCCESSFULLY

One of the dreams of most aspiring judoka is to open a school of their own someday and run it successfully. The prerequisites for opening a school are a shodan or higher black belt and a Senior Instructor License (or Certified International Instructor License). Your next step is choosing a location. Most judo schools in the country (73 percent, according to a Seibukan-kai survey) are operated out of colleges, universities, high schools, and YMCAs. The remainder (27 percent) are storefront schools. Of these storefront operations, 65 percent are schools that teach other martial arts as well (such as karate or jujutsu), while the remaining 35 percent are solely judo establishments.

So the first decision to make involves selecting a location. This appendix cannot get into the accounting, managing, and other operations of such a venture. What I will get into, however, applies whether your dojo will be a storefront or a YMCA establishment: *generating publicity to make the public aware that you exist.*

NEWS RELEASES

The newspapers and magazines that you read contain: news, editorial features, and advertising. In addition to the so-called hard news, you will find a variety of soft news features about companies, career advancements, etc. In fact, many of these articles are illustrated with portraits and product shots to clarify the soft news at hand. Where does the paper get these so-called soft news pieces? Simply from the individuals who are featured in the articles. Large companies employ someone to write these PR pieces; others employ PR agencies to do it for them.

As the sensei in your judo dojo, you too can benefit from publicity about you and your organization. Such publicity is not that difficult to obtain if you offer good instruction and can produce good students (these points are more important than being good yourself).

Remember that publicity is only part of a total promotion campaign for your dojo. Promotions includes all activities you engage in to inform your potential students about your dojo and the service you have to offer (quality instruction). Of the two main types of promotion, advertising and publicity, advertising is where money is spent directly. Advertising includes the purchase of media space in newspapers, yellow pages, store fronts, radio, and TV. Publicity, on the other hand, costs you time and effort but no real money. Publicity works to create word-of-mouth business that—when backed up with advertising—will bring your students in.

HOW TO GET PUBLICITY

Good publicity about you and your dojo will do one or more of several things:

1. It creates credibility. When one person says something good about you, others tend to believe it.
2. It implies an endorsement of you and your dojo.
3. It creates interest in you and your product (in this case judo). This interest will bring new students to your door.

How do you generate publicity? This can be done in several ways, but perhaps the most important aspect of this is your image. In a word, your image is your reputation. Everything you do helps to create your image. There are several things you can do to create a favorable image:

1. *Appearance:* The type of letterhead you use, your dojo's cleanliness, the quality of your equipment, the conditions of your mats, etc., reflect the quality of your establishment.
2. *Behavior:* This involves *your* personal behavior and appearance. A careless, sloppy appearance will make one look unprofessional. Keep your *gi* clean, your hair neat, etc.
3. *Treatment:* Every potential student expects to be treated with some amount of courtesy. All too often the strict discipline of student/teacher makes the sensei feel he can treat his potential customers as being less than human. *Every student—regardless of proficiency—deserves to be respected as a person. Remember this!*

A second way to generate publicity, apart from your image, involves the media.

One way is to hold a grand opening of your school. This can involve press conferences, TV coverage, etc. It is best to contact a PR person in your area for planning and budgeting such an event.

On a smaller scale is the press release. This involves writing a small release (in the way you wish it to read in print) on the event/happening you want publicity for: your grand opening, your new promotion to sandan, your team's winning a major regional event, etc.

To decide what kind of information you should include in your release, use the following checklist.

- Community relations projects (rape prevention programs, etc.)
- New equipment, new ranks (belts)
- New location
- Winning tournaments
- Testing and promoting of your students
- Contests you are running
- Public demonstrations (shows of your ability and that of your students)
- Unusual uses of judo, such as a student's surviving a street confrontation through the use of judo techniques
- Personnel changes, such as a new black belt teacher, etc.
- Awards that you receive or bestow

To prepare your first press release, you need a letterhead. This should be arranged with a local printer and should be designed with your image in mind. This release should be prepared on your letterhead. The use of blank typing paper is considered amateurish and may well cause your release to be discarded. Make extra copies of your release for future use. By making changes in copy of a previous release to fit new circumstances, you have in essence created a new release.

Your release should contain a heading, a suggested title, the body, and an ending. All heading information should be typed single-space. The rest of the release should be typed double-space with 1½-inch margins at left, right, and bottom. This allows room for the editor to edit and make corrections.

Provide a suggested title for each release you submit. The title should, in essence, tell what the release is about and capture the editor's attention. To get ideas, study your local newspaper and examine its titles and headlines.

Next, drop down about four spaces from your title and prepare the body of the release. Your first paragraph should tell the most important information in the release: *who, what, when, where,* and *why.* This paragraph should be able to stand alone since it just might if there isn't enough editorial space to print the entire release. The other paragraphs should add support information to the first paragraph. Each succeeding paragraph becomes less essential to the release, so if the editor has to cut down on a few paragraphs, it won't hurt your publicity release since the major information will have been presented.

STRATEGY IN THE MARKETPLACE

When preparing news releases, be sure to submit pieces that will be of interest to most people. Use quotes when possible to add interest to the piece. You can always quote yourself as if you were giving an interview to a reporter.

Now that you have your first release, research and identify the media that cover your market area. Be sure to include *all* newspapers and TV and radio stations in your area. Look for specialized publications that pinpoint your marketplace (such as a town paper or a "pennysaver"). National magazines like *Black Belt, Inside Karate,* and even *Official Karate* are interested in all martial arts (thus, judo), so sending releases to these publications will increase your reputation in your art. *Official Karate* has a gossip column (so to speak) for each section of the country ("Eye on East Coast," "Southern Exposure," "Western Wrapup," etc.). The magazine is always looking for release info.

Submit photos with releases as these often add interest and life to an otherwise dull editorial feature. Publicity portraits, action photos that clearly show your face, and the like should be printed on glossy 8-by-10 paper with a ¼-inch border.

Keep in mind that PR photos that are given to the media are not paid for and are not returned. On plain paper, type several sentences that tell who, what, when, where, and why about the subject in the picture. This caption, with your name, address, and phone number, is taped to the back of the print. Be sure to protect the photo by mailing it in a sturdy envelope marked *PHOTOS, DO NOT BEND.*

All submissions to different editors and news directors should be mailed out at the same time. It is not professional for someone to receive a press release two days after another source received the info. Generally, it is not wise to deliver press releases in person. Your visit will be a disruption to an already busy schedule. Also, *never* try to give the information over the phone. Instead, you can call a few days after you've mailed the release to make sure it was received and as a way to alert the media of its existence.

Remember too that a release is news and not a sales letter. If it is too commercial, it will probably be rejected. Be patient in your efforts to have releases published. Business news and similar items are used as fillers and may be preempted by advertising and editorial copy.

A final note to keep in mind: Running a successful judo dojo, whether it be through the YMCA or through a commercial school, requires that the public knows you exist. Make publicity an important part of your total promotional plan and an equal partner with your advertising plan. Together, paid advertising and publicity will sow the seeds of future business opportunities. And this means more students to live and grow through the art and science of judo—the "gentle way."

APPENDIX V:
TOWARD NUTRITIONAL AWARENESS

The problem facing most judoka is that they do not approach their judo training as a complete holistic activity. They train hard several days a week, but away from the dojo everything seems to fall apart. Simply put: You can't make it work in the dojo if you don't make it work every moment of your life.

This is a very hard rule to follow, but when it is adhered to, the judoka develops not only superior physical/mental techniques but also a high level of wellness.

This wellness comes about through nutritional awareness. In my first book, *The Complete Book of Judo*, we discuss the basic nutritional questions by examining vitamins, minerals, and other nutritional considerations. What I would like to discuss here is the concept of total nutritional awareness that leads the judoka to a high level of wellness.

To become nutritionally aware, follow the guidelines below. Remember, when looking over these guidelines, that many will label them as "health nut" activities and will ignore them. This is too bad since the key to consis-tent championship-level judo performance lies in these guidelines.

1. *Go for natural foods.* Although they are harder to obtain than commercially processed foods, natural foods have a proven record of health benefits and are well worth the extra trouble to obtain them. Some of the more recommended foods for the judoka are:

- *Soybeans.* Soybean sprouts have an enzyme called *invertase*, which can convert stored carbohydrates into quick, usable energy. This is of special interest to hard-training judoka. Also, all soybean products are good substitutions for meat products. Namely, tofu, tempeh, and miso.
- *Fresh fruits and raw vegetables.* Whole fruits and vegetables are better than the juices, which lose something in the heating process for canning and bottling.
- *Yogurt.* An extremely beneficial food that helps digestion and helps the body fight infection. It is best when homemade and

sweetened with honey and/or fresh fruit.

- *Garlic.* Nature's wonder food that rids the body of infections and lowers the blood pressure. When mixed with parsley (or when parsley is eaten after garlic), the pungent odor in the mouth from this wonder food is practically nonexistent.
- *Honey.* Called by many "nature's perfect food," honey contains a large amount of vitamins and essential minerals, including all the essential amino acids.
- *Apple cider vinegar.* Authority Dr. Jarvis's favorite tonic, apple cider vinegar helps to fight body infection and is a wonderful healing agent. Try a couple of teaspoons in a glass of water (three times a day) or use it as a dressing for salads once a day.
- *Nutritional yeast.* Contains all the major B complex vitamins. Some varieties are also 50-percent protein.
- *Wheat germ.* Removed from processed foods to add to shelf life, wheat germ is a major source of E and B vitamins as well as trace minerals.
- *Watermelon.* An excellent diuretic for removing body waste products. One of my judo sensei recommended watermelon highly as a postworkout treat.
- *Sunflower seeds.* Loaded with vitamins, minerals, and trace elements, sunflower seeds are rich in fiber and are an excellent source of polyunsaturated oil high in linoleic acid. They are easy to digest and can be an excellent preworkout treat (if eaten about one hour before a workout).
- *Bran.* An excellent source of fiber, it is recommended as perhaps the best food for a healthy digestive tract.

2. *Vary your diet.* Choose different types of food during the week.

3. *Avoid dangerous foods and food additives.* The prevalence of known and suspected carcinogenic elements entering our food supply as artificial colors, additives, preservatives, stabilizers, and other chemicals is well established. Nitrates, a leading factor in cancer of the colon, are found in most bacon, sausage, luncheon meats, and frankfurters; and petroleum derivatives such as BHA and BHT, and artificial flavors and colors are standard ingredients in so many of our foods. Don't use counterfeit products; they can do you no good but may cause you serious grief.

4. *Don't use refined or processed foods.* Examples are packaged cereals, candies, commercial ice creams, colas, etc. They consist mostly of empty calories devoid of nutritional value, including vitamins, minerals, and amino acids. According to an AMA survey (1983) processed foods make up 80 percent of the average American diet. Since the average individual likes some of these processed foods (myself included), the key is to cut down and make them as little as 10–20 percent of your diet.

5. *Learn to dislike refined sugar.* Think of it this way: sugar provides added calories—that's it! It is absorbed directly into the bloodstream, requiring immediate insulin treatment from the pancreas, which upsets the endocrine balance within the body. Refined sugar is highly concentrated; it lacks other food factors or proteins needed for metabolic processes to function properly. The body therefore must draw on its own reserves to metabolize the sugar, which causes a loss of vitamins B_1, B_2, B_6, niacin, magnesium, cobalt, and other nutrients. A buildup of lactic acid can occur if sugar is not metabolized completely.

6. *Avoid alcohol, coffee, tea, and other addictive drugs.* For most this is easy to say but *very* hard to make a reality. Each of these items will hinder professional judo performance as well as high-level wellness, which is one of the primary goals of judo (*rentai-ho*, perfect physical condition, from judo's Three Cultured Principles). Try herbal teas, which are good for you as well as help the body rebalance itself.

7. *Be sure to get high-quality protein.* When foods contain all eight essential amino acids (there are 20 amino acids, and the body can produce all but eight; therefore, they must be supplied from another source) they are called high-quality protein foods. Meats, vegetables, and seafood contain all eight (some vegetables contain only a few, so they must be

eaten in complement to each other to secure all eight). Always give yourself variety in getting your amino acids. One day get them with chicken, another day fish, and still another day (the preferred method) vegetables.

8. *Enjoy fresh fruit and uncooked vegetables every day.* The fresher your food, the more enzymes and nutrients are in them.

9. *Try to get high-fiber roughage every day.* The best way to do this is with a refreshing salad for lunch or supper. Roughage cleans the intestinal tract and helps prevent colon cancer.

10. *Start every day with a good breakfast.* While you are at it, enjoy a good lunch and supper too. Skipping meals (except when fasting or when you just aren't hungry) often leads to food distractions during the day. Don't leave the table stuffed, but don't go away hungry. Remember, be aware that little or no breakfast can cause dangerously low blood sugar levels (this is natural body-produced sugar—not refined sugars), interfering with concentration and body functioning.

You should always take a personal approach to nutrition since what works for some will not work as well for others. Become aware of yourself and your needs and be religious about fulfilling those needs. The reward will be an active and full judo career and a life filled with happiness. High-level wellness will make you totally alive and happy all your long healthy life.

APPENDIX VI:
FOOTNOTES FOR FURTHER INFORMATION

The following terms and techniques are discussed in more detail in *The Complete Book of Judo.*

Refer to the pages listed below for further information.

1. Ukemi-waza methods to prevent injury: 56–65.
2. Meditative posture: 42.
3. Breathing control: 43–45.
4. Flexibility exercises: 48–58.
5. Yoga exercises: 28–42.
6. Two-man squats: 50–51.
7. Two-man belt exercises: 54–57.
8. Isometrics: 56–57.
9. Holistic approach to judo: 23–24.
10. Neck exercises: 54–55.
11. Gokyo-waza throwing system: 66–115.
12. Kuzushi: 16.
13. Tsukuri: 19.
14. Kake: 19.
15. C grip: 20.
16. Seoinage: 80–81.
17. Ko-uchi-gari: 82–83.
18. Holding techniques: 117–133.
44. Hiza-guruma: 70.
45. De-ashi-harai: 68.
46. O-uchi-gari: 78.
47. Tai-oshi: 86.
48. Ko-soto-gake: 90.
49. Ushiro-goshi: 112.
50. Koshi-guruma: 84.
51. Hane-goshi: 94.
52. Utsuri-goshi: 104.
53. Sukui-nage: 102.
54. Uchi-mata: 90.

19. Kesa-gatame: 118.
20. Kami-shiho-gatame: 120.
21. Yoko-shiho-gatame: 128–31.
22. Juji-gatame: 124.
23. Kata-ha-jime: 130.
24. Kata-gatame: 118.
25. Gyaku-juji-jime: 128.
26. Waki-gatame: 126.
27. Jita Kyoei: 141.
28. Kata-guruma: 98.
29. Uki-goshi: 72.
30. Harai-goshi: 88.
31. Tsuri-komi-goshi: 84.
32. Okuri-ashi-harai: 86.
33. Sasae-tsuri-komi-ashi: 72–73.
34. Uchi-mata: 90.
35. Tomoe-nage: 80.
36. Ura-nage: 112.
37. Jigotai-kumi-kata: 20.
38. Sumi-gaeshi: 100.
39. Yoko-gake: 114.
40. Yoko-guruma: 110.
41. Uki-waza: 100.
42. O-soto-gari: 74.
43. Jigotai posture: 20.
55. Ippon seoinage: 90.
56. Kata-gatame: 118.
57. Hadaka-jime choking position: 128.
58. O-goshi: 76.
59. Okuri-eri-jime: 130.
60. Uki-otoshi: 106.
61. Yoko-wakare: 110.
62. United States Judo Federation and United States Judo Association requirements: 145.
63. Minimum age chart—judo ranks: 146.

ABOUT THIS BOOK

ABOUT THE AUTHOR

A member of the prestigious American Society of Classical Judoka, and a member of its advisory board, George R. Parulski, Jr., has compiled a multifaceted career in the martial arts. Born in Rochester, New York, in 1954, he has become recognized worldwide as an authority on martial arts culture, history, and philosophy through his many articles and books in the field.

He is a frequent contributor to *Official Karate, Inside Karate, Warriors,* and *Black Belt* magazines. He has also authored several books on the martial arts: *A Path to Oriental Wisdom* (Ohara Publications), *The Complete Book of Judo* (Contemporary Books, Inc.), *The Art of Karate Weapons* (Contemporary), *The Secrets of Kung-fu* (Contemporary), and *Taekwon-do* (with Mark McCarthy; Contemporary).

Parulski began his martial arts training in 1963, studying judo and karate under James D. Mounts and Frank L. Lane (the latter awarded him his first black belt). He holds black belt ranks in judo (godan from the American Society of Classical Judoka; yondan from All-Japan Seibukan Martial Arts and

Ways Association), shotokan karate (yondan, Japan Karate Association, American Karate Federation), goju-ryu karate (sandan, Zen Nippon Goju-ryu Karate-do Kai, All Japan Seibukan Martial Arts and Ways Association), aiki-jujutsu (*menkyo* rank, All-Japan Seibukan Martial Arts and Ways Association), *iai-do* (*shodan*, Eisho-ji, School of Zen), *shaolin* kung-fu and *tai ch'i ch'uan* (white-sash teacher level—Chinese Kung-fu/Wu-shu Federation), and teaching certification in yoga (Eisho-ji, School of Zen).

In addition to his black belt certifications, Parulski holds International Instructor Certification (Dai-Nippon Seibukan Budo/Bugei-Kai) in shotokan karate, Tenshin-shin'yo-ryu aiki-jujutsu, classical Kodokan judo, and goju-ryu karate-do, and a Senior Instructor License from the American Society of Classical Judoka. He is also a certified herbalist with the Chinese Kung-fu/Wu-shu Federation.

In addition to his school training, Parulski lived for three summers at the Eisho-ji, Zen Community (Campbell, New York), where he studied iai-do, yoga, and Zen philosophy.

Aside from studying the martial arts, Parulski competed heavily in the late 1960s and early 1970s. He won first place (weapons division/with sword) at the 1974 Pro-Am Goodwill Karate Championships (Florida—six countries competing), first place in the 1974 AAU East Coast Judo Championships, and, most recently, two firsts (Master Kata Division/Black Belt Weapons) and one second place (lightweight fighting) at the 1983 American Karate Federation's Grand Nationals. In addition to these major wins, Parulski has taken some 30 titles in his five years of competing (1969–1974).

He currently directs the Yama-ji, School of Traditional Martial Arts, is the USA President for the All-Japan Seibukan Martial Arts and Ways Association (Dai-Nippon Seibukan Budo/Bugei-Kai), and instructs a philosophy and martial arts program at St. John Fisher College.

He makes his home in Webster, New York, with his wife, Carolyn, and their children, Jaclyn and Charlie.

ABOUT THE ASSISTANTS

Bill "Rocket Man" Rourke

W. P. (Bill) Rourke was born in Brantford, Ontario, Canada, in 1942. Educated in Rochester, New York, Rourke holds a Bachelor of Science degree in industrial marketing from the Rochester Institute of Technology.

In addition to holding certification in judo and yoga, Rourke was a wrestling champion in Long Island, New York, and in Toronto, Ontario, Canada.

Rourke has been labeled "Rocket Man" by his peers because of his unique leaping abilities as applied to ukemi-waza (breakfalls). His major asset in judo is his ability to stay on his feet. As one of his peers puts it, "He has incredible rooting power."

He makes his home in Rochester, New York, with his wife, Pat, and their daughters, Ashley and Brooke.

ABOUT THE TECHNICAL ADVISOR

The founder and president of the American Society of Classical Judoka, Isao Obato holds a seventh-degree black belt (shichidan) in judo, with black belt certification in such arts as jo-jutsu (staff fighting), iai-jutsu/iai-do (sword drawing), ken-jutsu/kendo (sword fighting), aikido, aiki-jutsu, and jujutsu. He also is an accomplished yogi and author of material on Zen philosophy.

Born in 1934 in Osaka, Japan, Obato began his study of judo at the age of 10 from the Kodokan headquarters in Japan. In addition to this, he resided for several years at the Enkaku-ji Zen monastery. Preferring the more spiritual end of the martial arts, Obato received ranks from the aikido hombu and the *butokukai* in traditional bugei (martial arts).

Committed to seeing judo recognized as a martial art and a means of physical/spiritual cultivation, Obato founded the American Society of Classical Judoka, which is becoming recognized around the world as judo's nonsport certification body.

He makes his home in Phoenix, Arizona, with his wife, Mako, and their children, Robert, Frank, Brian, and Carrie.

Rob "The Gentleman" Horowitz

Born in Rochester, New York, Horowitz holds certification in judo and an *oku-eri* level certification in Tenshin-shin'yo-ryu aiki-jutsu. Schooled at Duke University (Durham, North Carolina) and St. John Fisher College (Rochester, New York), Rob devotes nearly full-time to his study of *budo* (martial ways).

In addition to martial arts Horowitz enjoys such activities as reading, writing, drawing, running, camping, and weight training. He is an accomplished musician, versed in piano, trumpet, and bass.

His strong points in judo are his speed and his power. As one of his fellow judoka observed, "He moves in and out of a throw so quickly that it is hard to initiate a counterattack." Perhaps the reason for his effectiveness in judo is his high rank in aiki-jujutsu. Its circular method of dissipation of oncoming force gives Horowitz an edge that he exploits on the mat.

He makes his home in Rochester, New York, living his life by the code of bushido. A rare judoka, indeed!

ABOUT THE SUMI-E ARTIST

Carolyn Parulski was born in Rochester, New York, in 1952. She attended the Rochester Institute of Technology for art and is certified by the Eisho-ji School of Zen (Campbell, New York) as an accomplished *sumi-e* artist. Her work has appeared in such martial arts publications as *Official Karate, Inside Kung-fu,* and *Black Belt.* Her work has also appeared in such general-interest publications as *New Thought, Orion, Rosicrucian Digest,* and *Probe the Unknown.* She masterfully struck the cover for her husband's best-selling philosophy book, *A Path to Oriental Wisdom* (Ohara Publications, Inc.), as well as supplying the interior illustrations.

She makes her home in Webster, New York, with her husband, George, and their children, Jaclyn and Charlie.

ABOUT THE CALLIGRAPHY ON THE BACK COVER

Translating as "budo (martial way) soul," the work was done by Sensei Otake of the Tenshin Shoden Katori Shinto-ryu. Reprinted with permission from the All-Japan Seibukan Martial Arts and Ways Association. The square seals are Master Otake's personal seals.

INDEX